AF485850

African Myths

Captivating Stories, Folk Tales, Gods, and Goddesses of African Mythology

Free Bonus from Captivating History (Available for a Limited time)

Table of Contents

Introduction

African myth and folklore have a rich tapestry of tales about gods and spirits, giants and monsters, animals and human beings, magic and the ordinary. Each African culture has its own values and ways of seeing the world, but the stories that come out of these cultures all participate in the human desire to explain why we are here, why the world is the way it is, and to see to it that right is upheld and evil thoroughly punished.

The first part of the book contains creation stories from the Yoruba of Nigeria, the Khoisan of South Africa, and the Efik of Nigeria and Cameroon. In these stories, gods, spirits, animals, and people work together to make the world what it is.

In the second part of the book, we meet a series of giants and monsters, not all of whom are evil. For example, the stories of Untombinde, from the Zulu people of South Africa, and of Gihilihili, from the Tutsi people of Rwanda and Botswana, each show that what might seem monstrous on the surface may not, in fact, be anything evil and that it is necessary to look beneath the surface to see the truth of things.

Damsels in distress are the main characters of the tales in the third part. One tale from the Kikuyu people of Kenya, and one from the Berber of Morocco, are about two young women whom each find themselves in mortal peril. In the tale from Kenya, the peril is brought upon the young woman by external forces, while the heroine of the Berber tale gets herself into soup and needs to be helped out of it.

The final portion of this book is devoted to heroes who conquer not by strength of arms but through cleverness. The tricksters in the stories from Africa's east coast and Libya each have special magical powers that help them defeat their enemies, but the hero of the Ugandan story of Walukaga, the blacksmith, relies on good advice from an unlikely source.

Readers familiar with African folklore may wonder why this volume has so few animal tales. Although tales featuring the exploits and foibles of animal characters are certainly an important part of African folklore, this book concentrates more on stories about human beings, so only a few of these stories involve animal characters as main participants. Even so, the people in these stories are all placed in simultaneously wondrous and harrowing situations, showing that the world can be both a more complicated and more beautiful place than first meets the eye.

Part I: Beginnings

The Creation of the World (Yoruba, Nigeria)

This Yoruba tale from Nigeria explains how the world came to be. Instead of a single creator-god doing all the work, several Orishas, or divine spirits, work together. Also, in this particular tale, the sky and marshy earth are taken as givens; what is being created is a place for people and animals to live, and the people and animals themselves.

This tale is also a just-so story explaining why disability exists in the world and how people learned to make sacrifices to the Orishas. The city created by the god Olodumare is called Ife; thus, this story is the mythological origin tale of Ile-Ife, the oldest city in Nigeria and the holy city of traditional Yoruba religion.

How the Land Was Made

Long ago, before there were people or animals, there was only the sky above and a vast expanse of water and marshy places down below. The god Olodumare ruled the sky, and the goddess Olokun ruled the waters. Now, Olodumare had a son named Obatala. Often, Olodumare would look down at the marshy waters from his place up in the sky and wonder what would happen if someone were to change the world below; if someone were to make hills and mountains, plains and valleys. He wondered what would happen if the world had people and animals and birds to live on the land. For a very long time, Obatala gazed upon the waters and wondered about these things.

Finally, Obatala could stand it no longer.

He went to Olodumare and said, "I think the world needs to have more things in it than it already does. It needs hills and mountains, plains and valleys. It needs people and animals and birds to live in it. I ask your permission to go down and make these things."

Olodumare stroked his chin and replied, "That is a very ambitious undertaking, and I think it is worth accomplishing, but I cannot help you. Go and see my other son, Orunmila. He is very wise and will know exactly what you must do."

Obatala sought out Orunmila and told him what he wanted to do and that he had Olodumare's blessing.

"Oh, yes, I can certainly help you," Orunmila said. "Let me cast a divination to see what you will need." Orunmila made his divination, and when he was done, he said, "You will need several things to accomplish your task. First, you will need a golden chain to lower yourself from here to the world below. Then you will need a snail shell full of sand, a white hen, a black cat, and a palm nut."

Obatala thanked Orunmila for his help. Then he went looking for the gold with which to make the chain. He asked Orunmila whether he had any gold he might use, and Orunmila gladly gave him what he had. Obatala went to his other brother, the Orisha named Eshu, and Eshu gladly gave him some of his own gold. Obatala went to each Orisha in turn, and when he had explained what the gold was wanted for, they gladly gave him what he asked.

When Obatala had spoken to everyone who lived in the sky, he took the gold to the metalsmith and said, "I need a golden chain that will go from here all the way down to the waters below. Can you make that for me?"

"Oh, yes, indeed I can," the smith replied. "But you don't have enough gold here."

"Never fear. Make the chain as long as you can with the gold you have. I will see to the rest."

After a time, a messenger came to Obatala from the smith, saying that the golden chain was ready. Obatala went to the smithy and saw how beautiful and finely wrought the chain was, and he was very grateful for the smith's work.

"But there's only one thing missing," Obatala said. "Please can you take off some of the links at one end to make a hook? The chain won't do what I need it for without a hook."

The smith gladly took some of the links and made a hook, and when it was fastened to the end of the chain, Obatala was very glad indeed. He went to the edge of the sky and attached the hook to it, and then let the rest of the chain uncoil. The chain went down, down, down toward the water. The chain was so long that Obatala thought it would never stop uncoiling, but then suddenly, it was done, and Obatala saw that there was still some distance between the end of the chain and the surface of the water. Just as he pondered how he might solve this problem and whether he would hurt himself if he climbed to the very end of the chain and let go, Orunmila came walking up with a big bag in his hands.

"Here are the other things you need," Orunmila said. "In this bag is a snail shell full of sand, a white hen, a black cat, and a palm nut."

"Oh, thank you!" Obatala said. "Now I may start my journey."

Obatala slung the bag over his shoulder and began climbing down the chain. The farther he got from the sky, the darker it became. And out of the darkness came the sound of rushing water and waves crashing about. Obatala climbed all the way down to the bottom of the chain, where he realized that he had no idea how much farther down the water actually was: It was much too dark for him to see anything.

Just as he was beginning to despair that his plan would never work, he heard Orunmila's voice calling to him from far up in the sky. "Take out the snail shell and scatter the sand on the water."

Obatala did as Orunmila told him to do.

Then Orunmila said, "Take out the hen and drop her onto the sand."

Obatala dropped the hen onto the sand from the snail shell. The hen began to happily scratch at the sand, scattering it hither and thither, and soon a great mass of dry land extended across the waters. Because the hen was scratching this way and that and not thinking much about what she was doing, some of the sand piled up higher in some places than in others, and this is why there are hills and valleys and flat places on the land today.

Once the land had spread across the waters, Obatala saw that he could safely jump from the end of the chain onto the land. There he planted the palm nut. Soon the palm nut sprouted, and then it became a tree. It grew and put forth fruit and seeds, and from the seeds, more trees sprang up, and this was the beginning of all the plants that live upon the land. Obatala cut down some of the palm trees to build himself a hut to live in, and the black cat was his companion. Obatala called the place he was living Ife, and that place is still there today.

After a time, Olodumare became curious about whether Obatala had been successful with his plans. He told Agemo the chameleon to climb down the golden chain and find out what Obatala had been up to and then return and give a full report. Agemo obediently went down the chain, where he found Obatala living with his cat and hen in a little hut made of palm trees on land that stretched far and wide; land that had hills and plains and mountains.

Agemo went to Obatala and said, "Your father Olodumare sent me to see how things are with you and whether you were successful with your plans."

"Look about you," Obatala said, gesturing to the land and all the plants that were growing on it. "I have been very successful indeed. There is one thing, though... It's rather dark here. At first, it didn't bother me much, but I would really prefer to have more light. Please return to Olodumare and ask whether he might provide me with more light because that is one thing I cannot make for myself."

Agemo bid farewell to Obatala and climbed up the chain back into the sky. Agemo went to Olodumare and told him all that Obatala had accomplished.

Olodumare was very impressed with Agemo's tale and said, "Is there anything else that Obatala requires? For he has accomplished a great feat, and I wish to reward him well."

"Yes," Agemo replied. "He says it is too dark down there on his new land. He would like some more light, please."

"Certainly," Olodumare said.

And so it was that Olodumare took some light and fashioned it into a ball. He fixed the ball of light in the sky, and this is how the sun was made.

Obatala Creates Human Beings

When Obatala saw the sun Olodumare had made for his land, he was very content, so he lived in his hut with his cat and hen for some time longer. Eventually, Obatala became restless.

"All this land and all these plants are well and good," he said. "But I really do wish there were more creatures like me, who can walk and talk and think and make things. I think it's time I made some creatures like that."

Obatala dug up some soft, pliable clay and began to make little figures out of it. He made the figures look like him, with two arms, two legs, and a head on top. He made several of these and set them aside to dry, and when this was done, he found that he was very thirsty. He made some palm wine for himself to drink, and since he was thirsty, he drank a great quantity very quickly. Unfortunately, in a short time, Obatala was quite drunk, but he paid this no mind because he was no longer thirsty. In his drunken state, he resumed making little figures out of clay, but they were unlike the ones he had made earlier. These new figures were misshapen because Obatala was drunk and could not see clearly. Some of the new figures were missing limbs. Some had one leg longer than the other. Some had crooked bodies. Some had heads that were the wrong size. But Obatala set them down to dry next to the others anyway, not noticing what he had done.

When Obatala felt that he had made enough figures, he looked up into the sky and said, "Olodumare, please hear me. I have made little figures out of clay. I want them to be people to live with me on the land I have made because I want there to be creatures like me who can walk and talk and think and make things. Olodumare, will you breathe life into my little clay figures, please?"

Olodumare gladly breathed life into the little clay figures and soon, there sprang up a bustling village around Olodumare's solitary hut. By the time the village had been built, the palm wine had worn off, and Obatala noticed that some of the people were misshapen and had difficulty doing their tasks.

"Oh, no!" Obatala cried. "In my drunkenness, I made creatures that were misshapen. I regret this very much. I will be the special protector of all people whose bodies and minds are not perfectly made."

And Obatala keeps that promise still.

Obatala gave the new people many gifts. He gave them crops for food and tools for farming and hunting. He also taught the people how to use the tools and raise the crops. He did not want his children to go hungry.

When Obatala saw his new people thriving, he decided it was time for him to return to his place in the sky.

"Do not fear," he told the people. "I have given you everything you need to live on this land. All will be well. But for now, I need to return to my father's house. Farewell."

The Great Flood

Up in the heavens, the other Orishas constantly asked Obatala to tell the story of how he had made the land and people. They wanted to know everything about the plants Obatala had made and the village of Ife, where the new people were living. Obatala gladly told them everything they wanted to know, and the Orishas were impressed with all his deeds. Some were so impressed that they wanted to go down and live on the land among the people. Olodumare gave them permission to go, along with the instruction that they should help the people whenever asked.

"For you have great power," Olodumare said, "and the people do not. Therefore, you should befriend them always."

The Orishas agreed, so they went down and found good places to live on the land that Obatala had made.

However, one Orisha was angry and jealous of what Obatala had done, and that was the water goddess Olokun. She was angry that Obatala had created a land, plants, and people on top of her waters without even asking and even angrier that some of the Orishas had gone down to the land and made parts of it their own.

"Obatala and the others have done me a great wrong. They have no respect for me. I will show them which of us is the more powerful," Olokun said.

And so, Olokun caused all the waters to rise and create a great flood. The waters crept into the houses and onto the lanes and byways. They rushed into the fields, submerging the people's crops. The people ran to the hills to escape the rushing waters, but many of them were not swift enough, and so they perished in the deluge. They cried out from the tops of the hills to Obatala, but he was living in the sky and was too far away to hear them.

When they found that Obatala did not hear them, they pleaded with Eshu, one of the Orishas who had come down to live on the land.

"Great Eshu," they cried, "save us from this terrible flood! Use your great power to save us!"

"If you want help," Eshu replied, "you must pray and make a sacrifice first."

The people took a goat and sacrificed it to Obatala. They prayed and prayed for Obatala to come and save them, but still, the waters did not recede.

"What have we done wrong?" the people asked Eshu.

"You have made a sacrifice and prayed to Obatala, and that is good," Eshu said. "But if you want someone to take your message to Obatala up in the sky, you need to sacrifice and pray to them, too."

The people then took another goat, and this time, they sacrificed it to Eshu while saying many prayers to him.

When Eshu was satisfied with the sacrifice and the prayers, he said, "Now I will go."

Thus, he climbed the golden chain all the way back up into the sky, where he told Obatala about the flood.

"Oh, this is terrible news!" Obatala cried. "My people must be saved, but I don't know what to do. Maybe Orunmila can help me. He is always very wise."

Obatala went to Orunmila and told him about the flood and Olokun's anger and jealousy.

"Yes, that is very bad," Orunmila said. "But have no fear. I know what must be done. Wait here, and I will see to it that all is set right."

Orunmila climbed down the golden chain. He turned the waters back and made the flooded places dry again. The people saw what Orunmila had done and gave him great praise.

"Stay with us!" they cried. "You are very powerful, and we need your help and protection!"

"I do not wish to stay here," Orunmila said. "But before I go, I will teach you many things that will help you."

Henceforth, Orunmila selected the wisest of the people and the Orishas who lived on the land. He taught them how to do divination and many other powerful things that would help them control the world they lived in. The people and the Orishas remembered everything Orunmila taught them, and they taught these arts to their children and their children's children.

And so it is today that the wise ones among the people have special skills and powers they can use to help others.

How the Sun Got Into the Sky
(*Khoisan, South Africa*)

This just-so story from the Khoisan people of South Africa explains how the sun got into the sky and why the moon waxes and wanes. In this story, the moon asks the sun to "leave the children the backbone." This likely refers to the "backbone of night," which is the name many South African people give the Milky Way.

There once was a time when the sun was not a bright orb in the sky. Instead, the sun was a patch of warmth and brightness that stayed under a man's armpit. Whenever the man lifted his arm, light and warmth would flow out, but it only brightened and warmed the place immediately around him. When he put his arm down, the light and warmth would cease, and so it was that for most of the time, the world was dark and cold.

An old woman went to a younger woman who had many children.

The old woman said, "Ask your children to go to the place where Sun-Armpit lives. Tell your children that they must grab hold of him very firmly and throw him up into the sky. Tell the children to say, 'Sun-Armpit, you must stay up there in the sky. Become a shining orb. Send light and warmth down onto the earth, for the people are unhappy that it is so dark and cold.'"

The younger woman called her children to herself and instructed them as the old woman told her to do. The children went very quietly to Sun-Armpit's house. They waited until he was asleep. Then they crept into his house and took hold of him very tightly.

They brought him out of his house and threw him bodily into the sky, saying, "Sun-Armpit! You must stay up there in the sky! Become a shining orb! Send light and warmth down onto the earth, for the people are unhappy that it is so dark and cold."

The children returned home and told their mother and the old woman, "We went to Sun-Armpit's house. We took hold of him very tightly and threw him into the sky. We told him to stay there and be a shining orb and send down light and warmth upon the earth."

Once Sun-Armpit had been thrown into the sky, he stayed there. He was thrown up into the sky as a man, but he became a shining orb that sent down light and warmth. Sun-Armpit stayed up in the sky with the moon. While the sun shone, it was day. When the sun went away, it was night.

One time, the sun and the moon quarreled, and the sun stabbed the moon with his knife. This is why the moon wanes—because he has been stabbed by the sun's knife. However, the moon always heals and becomes whole again.

When the sun stabbed the moon, the moon said, "Sun, leave the children the backbone!"

And the sun agreed to leave the children the backbone.

The people set out their rice to dry, and the sun's warmth dried it. The people saw the springbok, and the sun's light showed it to them. The people could see the food they were eating. They could see the roads they were walking. They could see the faces of their loved ones who came to visit.

How the Stars Were Made
(Efik, Nigeria, and Cameroon)

In this tale from West Africa, we learn that the stars and moon were not made through the power of Effion Obassi, the primary god of the Efik people, but rather through the generosity of Iku, the water chevrotain, and the action of a wayward breeze. (The water chevrotain is a small fanged deer that lives along streams and rivers in the tropical regions of Africa.)

The story also involves a structure called the Ekpe House, which is a building used by the Ekpe secret society. The society is devoted to the forest spirit of the same name. Only males are allowed to be members of the society, which is part of the culture of the Efik and a few other West African peoples. Members of the Ekpe society are usually inducted at puberty. The society contains a hierarchy of ranks that members can climb, and traditionally, the purpose of the society was to mete out justice. It also provides social status to its members. These societies still exist today.

Ebopp, the bush baby, and Mbaw, the dormouse, were good friends. One day, they decided that they would like to farm together, so they went looking for a good place to have their farm. They searched for many days, but finally, they found a place in the bush that no one else had claimed and looked like a good place to have a farm. They decided which part of the land belonged to Ebopp and which to Mbaw, and then they went to work right away, felling trees and clearing the land to plant their crops. This took two days, and at the end of the second day, they returned to their village.

The next day, they went back to their new farm.

"We must build an Ekpa Ntan before we do any more work," Ebopp said.

"Yes," Mbaw agreed. "That is the first thing we must do."

Thus, Ebopp and Mbaw built a small house with no walls in the place where they had decided their Ekpe House would be once the village was established. When this was done, they were very tired, so they went home and rested for two days.

On the third day, they went back to their new farm. This time they each worked their own land. At the end of the day, they were tired and hungry, so they went home, where they found their wives had cooked them a good meal. They ate together and then went to bed.

In the morning, they worked again, and their wives helped them. First, they planted plantains, and this work took two days. Then they planted yams, and this work took two days more, and then they were satisfied that their farms were complete.

Ebopp, Mbaw, and their wives went home to rest and have a meal. While Ebopp was eating, a messenger came from Obassi Osaw, the sky god. Obassi Osaw was the father of Ebopp's wife, Akpan Anwan.

The messenger said, "Ebopp, I would like to speak to you alone, please."

Akpan Anwan left the room.

When she was gone, the messenger said, "Ebopp, I bring you very bad news. Akpan Anwan's sister has died."

Ebopp was stricken with grief. He said to the messenger, "This is very bad news indeed. Please, on your way back to Obassi Osaw's house, will you please stop at my friend Mbaw's house and ask him to come here?"

The messenger gladly agreed, and when Mbaw arrived, Ebopp told him the bad news.

"Oh, that is terrible!" Mbaw said. "I grieve with you and your family. But what are we to do about the funeral? We only just started our farms. We'll never be able to hold a proper feast, and Obassi Osaw will never forgive you if you don't hold a proper feast."

"I know," Ebopp replied. "But I have to try. Please, will you go to Obassi Osaw and ask him to give me six days to make the preparations?"

Mbaw gladly agreed, and when he returned, he and Ebopp set about planning the funeral.

When they had decided how to proceed, Ebopp said, "I cannot wait any longer to tell my wife. She will wonder what we are doing and why, and she needs to know about her sister. My heart breaks knowing how she will grieve."

Ebopp then went to Akpan Anwan and told her that her sister was dead. Akpan Anwan wailed in her grief. Ebopp did his best to comfort her, but it was to no avail.

Then Ebopp said, "I told your father we would hold your sister's funeral feast in five days. You must be ready to travel to your father's house then."

Ebopp and Mbaw spent all their money on food for the feast, buying up every last plantain they could find.

When the last coin had been spent, Mbaw said, "What about palm wine and rum? We need the wine for the feast, and we must use the rum for the funeral libations."

"We have no more money," Ebopp replied. "We will have to ask our friends and neighbors whether they can lend us any palm wine or rum."

And so, Ebopp and Mbaw went to everyone in the village, but no one had any palm wine or rum to lend them, and the people who did have it wouldn't give it without payment. Next, Ebopp decided to go to where the makers of palm wine lived to see whether anyone there might help them. There, he found Iku, the water chevrotain. Ebopp told Iku that they needed palm wine and rum for the funeral and that no one would lend him some, and they had no money to buy any.

Iku said, "I'm sorry, but I don't have any palm wine or rum to give you."

Ebopp's shoulders slumped, and he looked like he was about to weep. Ebopp turned and began walking slowly away.

Iku watched him go and felt such pity for him that he called out, "Wait! I don't have any palm wine, but I might be able to help you another way."

Ebopp turned back around and saw Iku holding out two small, shining, round objects.

"I don't have any wine," Iku said. "But I do have my extra pair of eyes that I use to see in the dark. Maybe you can sell them and use that money to buy palm wine and rum."

Ebopp thanked Iku for his generosity and returned home.

The next day, Ebopp, Mbaw, and their wives packed up all the food they had bought for the feast, along with Iku's eyes, and set out for Obassi Osaw's village. When they arrived, they saw where Akpan Anwan's sister had been buried. Akpan Anwan dropped her burden and flung herself onto her sister's grave, weeping.

Obassi Osaw said, "Thank you for coming. What have you brought for the feast?"

"I have plantains enough for everyone, but I will need to buy palm wine and rum here," Ebopp replied.

"Very well," Obassi Osaw said, and so Ebopp and Mbaw put all the plantains into the Ekpe House until they were needed for the feast.

On the day of the feast, Ebopp and Mbaw gave the plantains to the people. There was enough for everyone to have one.

When the plantains had been eaten, Obassi Osaw said, "That was not enough food for a proper feast. If you cannot provide the customary funeral for your wife's sister, I will not allow your wife to go back to your village with you."

Ebopp went to Mbaw and told him what Obassi Osaw had said.

"Should I sell the eyes now?" Ebopp asked. "But I am concerned that if I sell them, I will not get a good price for them. There is famine here, and the people are already suffering. They won't be able to pay me what the eyes are worth."

"Yes, I agree," Mbaw replied. "But I think there is another solution. Get a mortar and pestle and a small cap. If we grind the eyes into small pieces, maybe you can sell them bit by bit and make more money that way."

"Oh, that is very wise! I will do as you say."

Ebopp got a mortar and pestle and ground the eyes into thousands of glittering fragments. He put the fragments into the cap.

When all was ready, Mbaw said, "Now you need to find out whether there's anyone who has enough food that he can sell you. Go start looking."

Ebopp followed Mbaw's advice, but no one had any food they could sell him, not even enough to be worth one tiny fragment of the shining eyes. Ebopp kept looking, and soon, he came to the house of Effion Obassi. When Effion Obassi opened the door, Ebopp could see that the house was full of all kinds of good food and also great stores of palm wine and rum.

Ebopp said, "I would like to buy all your food, palm wine, and rum. I can give you in exchange something that will make everyone bow down before you."

Effion thought for a moment about Ebopp's offer. Then he said, "I am willing to sell, but not everything. I will sell you only half."

Ebopp gladly accepted Effion's offer since even half of what was in the house would be more than enough for a grand funeral feast.

Ebopp handed the cap full of the eye fragments to Effion and said, "Here is your payment, but take care not to open the cap until after I have returned to my own home. At that point, you may open it, and all the people will bow down before you."

Ebopp brought the food, wine, and rum to Obassi Osaw's village, and there he held a great feast in his sister-in-law's honor. It was the best feast anyone had ever attended.

When it was over, Obassi Osaw said, "You have done well. You may return home with your wife."

Ebopp turned to his wife and Mbaw. "We should return home now. We should not spend the night here."

And so, they went home to their village.

When they got home, Ebopp sent a messenger to Effion Osaw.

The messenger said, "I come with a message from Ebopp. He has reached his home and says that you may now open the cap he gave you."

Now, the messenger had arrived when the sun had just set, but even though darkness was drawing nigh, Effion Obassi called together all of his village and said, "I have something wondrous to show you. Come and see!"

When all the people were gathered, Effion Obassi opened the cap, and inside were thousands of shining fragments, the fragments of Iku's eyes. No sooner had he opened the cap than a strong breeze blew through the town. The breeze lifted the fragments and scattered them everywhere so that the whole village was soon covered with tiny, glittering points of light.

"Gather them up!" Effion cried. "Gather them all up!"

The people went to work gathering up all the fragments. They worked and worked, but still, more shining fragments could be found. They discovered that they could only gather them at night because their sparkle was invisible during the day. After many nights, they had collected enough fragments to fill a box, and then a few nights later, they had so many fragments that the lid of the box could not be closed, and all of the fragments together in the box shone with a great light all their own. Then one night, when they were searching and searching for the last fragments and had nearly found them all, a great breeze came and scattered the fragments all over the village once more, and so the people had to go to work collecting them again.

Effion Obassi sent a messenger to Ebopp to ask whether Ebopp and his people could see the sparkling fragments at night. This is because Effion Obassi's village was in the sky, and this was a time when people could go back and forth between the sky and the earth. Ebopp said that he and his people could indeed see the sparkles and a great shining thing that grew in the sky every month and then diminished.

And this is why the stars are in the sky, and the moon grows and grows until it shines so brightly that we cannot see the stars. It is because Iku gave his eyes to Ebopp, who ground them up and gave them to Effion Obassi. The stars and the moon are made of the eye fragments, and the moon grows when Effion Obassi's people gather the fragments and put them in the box. This takes them a whole month, and at the end of the month, the breeze blows everything away again, and we see all the stars and no moon once again.

Part II: Giants and Monsters

The Giants, the Man, and the Cattle
(*Mensa, Eritrea*)

The Mensa people of Eritrea are one of many groups within the Tigre culture. The Tigre inhabit the northern part of Eritrea and historically have been farmers and cowherds. Cattle and cow herding largely feature in this story, in which a greedy wife sends her hapless husband out to steal some cattle from a nearby giant.

Another Mensa tale explains how the race of giants ended through a blessing gone wrong. The tale relates that when the giants realized that they were to die, they dug their own graves and set up their own tombstones, and so certain groupings of large, flat stones came to be known as giants' graves in Tigre folklore.

Once there was a race of giants who lived upon the earth in much the same way as human beings. The giants farmed the land and kept cattle. They had sons and daughters. They ate food and drew water from a well. One of these giants kept cattle and used to draw water for them using a vessel made from the whole hide of a bull. To draw the water, he would put one foot into a well that lay alongside the river on the same side as the pasture where the giant kept his cattle. This well was very deep and had a sandy bottom. With one foot in the well and the other in the cattle trough, the giant would lower the bull's hide down into the water, pull it up when it was full, and empty it into the trough.

To collect the milk from his cattle, the giant had another vessel made from the hide of an entire elephant, and his evening meal was an entire cow, roasted whole over a spit and eaten without being cut up into pieces. If the giant wanted wood for a fire, he did not need an ax or a saw: He would simply pull up whole trees by their roots and pile them up.

Now, not far from the giant's homestead lived a man with his wife. The man and his wife were very poor and often did not have enough to eat. The wife saw how many cattle the giant had, so she goaded her husband to steal them.

"Are you a man or a mouse?" she screeched. "Go steal some of that giant's cattle. He has plenty to spare. He won't even know that they're gone."

"Fine," the man said. "But if I don't come back with any cattle, then you may call me a mouse and go and get the cattle all by yourself."

The man went to the pasture where the giant kept his cattle. The man sat down at the edge of the pasture and watched the giant go about his day. He watched the giant milk his cattle into the huge vessel made from elephant skin. He watched the giant gather firewood by pulling up whole trees by their roots.

How am I ever going to steal cattle from a giant? the man wondered. *But I can't go home without trying, or my wife will think me a coward.*

Thus, the man sat and waited for his chance to do something.

After a time, the giant noticed the stranger sitting on the edge of his field and said, "Ho, there! Who are you, and where are you from?"

"Oh, I live hereabouts," the man replied, not wanting to give more information to the giant than he could help.

"Would you like some milk to drink?" the giant asked. "My cows make very fine milk."

"Yes, please," the man replied, and so the giant held out the elephant skin to the man, but it was too large for the man to drink from by itself.

"You are a funny little fellow," the giant said. "Here, let me help you."

The giant helped the man drink from the skin, and soon the man had had all the milk he could hold.

"Thank you. I am finished now," the man said.

"But you've hardly had anything at all!" the giant replied. "What you drank would not even fill half of my wife's thimble!"

Then the giant took the elephant-skin vessel and drank off all the milk in one draught.

After the giant had drunk the milk, he slaughtered a cow and roasted it over the fire he had made from the uprooted trees. When the meat was cooked, he tore off one of the hind legs and gave it to the man. The man ate all that he could hold, but it was only a tiny portion of the cow's haunch.

"What, have you no stomach at all?" the giant asked, and then he ate the rest of the cow by himself in two bites and the rest of the haunch that he had given to the man in one.

"Now, I must go home to my wife," the giant said, so he and the man bade their farewells to one another.

Fearing to go home without any of the giant's cattle, the man found himself a comfortable spot under a spreading tree, where he stayed awake long into the night, thinking of schemes by which he might be able to take at least some of the giant's cattle without getting himself killed.

In the morning, the giant drove his cattle back into the pasture. He saw that the man was still there and said, "Have you no home to go to? Why are you still here?"

"I have a home, but I am very poor," the man replied. "It's not worth it for me to go back there. I was hoping you would hire me to herd your cattle for you."

"I don't much see the point. You're too small to handle the vessel I use to milk my cows and too small to handle the vessel I use to draw water from the well. But still, no man should have to be poor. Here, take these five cattle and have them for your own."

And so, the giant gave the man five of his cattle, which the man drove triumphantly home to his wife.

"Look here!" the man said. "I have taken the giant's cows!"

And for a time, the man and woman lived together in contentment.

However, it was not to last. The wife was a greedy woman, and soon she began to think that they needed to increase their herd.

"Those five cows were a good start," the wife said. "But now I want all of the giant's herd, not just part of it. Go and get the rest of them."

"Why should I do that?" the man asked. "The giant was very generous to give us these cows. He didn't have to do that. He could have laughed at me and sent me on my way. Or even killed me!"

"Are you a man or a mouse?" the wife shrieked. "Go get the rest of those cattle and get them now."

Hence, the man had to go because he did not want his wife to think him a coward, and he especially did not want her to tell their neighbors that he was afraid.

When the man got to the giant's pasture, he sat down in the same place he had sat before.

Soon, the giant noticed him and said, "What, you again? Why are you here? What happened to the cattle I gave you?"

"Oh, it is a very sad tale," the man replied. "A great drought came to the place where I live, and then a murrain of livestock. All the cows you gave me died. I thought that maybe this time you would hire me to be your cowherd since I can't possibly ask you to give me more cows."

"You truly are an unfortunate fellow," the giant said, "and you are very small, but I suppose I can let you have a go at herding my cows. My daughter can go with you to help you. The first thing you need to do is to take this bull's hide and use it to draw water from the well. Mind that you don't let my daughter go into the well herself. Her duty is to watch the cattle while you draw the water."

And so, the man and the giant's daughter took the cattle out to pasture together.

Soon the day became hot, and the cattle were thirsty.

"Let us go down to the well to draw water for the cattle," the man said. "I'll draw the water, and you keep the cattle back until their trough is full."

The giant's daughter looked the man up and down and replied, "Are you sure you want to draw the water? You're awfully small. I don't think you're strong enough. Let me draw the water, and you watch the cattle."

"We can't do it that way. Your father said very clearly that I had to draw the water, and you were to watch the cattle and not go into the well, and I don't want to get into trouble."

"Very well. We'll try it your way."

The man and the giant's daughter drove the cattle down to the river. The man took the bull's hide vessel and lowered it into the water, but when the vessel was full, it was too heavy for the man to lift.

The giant's daughter saw him struggling and said, "Here, let's trade places. We'll just make sure to wipe off all the sand from the well, and my father won't know the difference."

Thus, the man watched the cows while the daughter drew the water and filled the trough. While the cows were drinking, the man helped the giant's daughter brush off all the sand.

When the pair went home with the cattle in the evening, the giant said, "So, my small friend, were you able to water the cattle properly, like I asked you to?"

"Certainly," the man replied. "It was no trouble at all."

"No trouble, eh? I'm not sure I believe that."

Hence, the giant called his daughter over to him and examined her for any traces of sand. Behind her ear, he found two grains of sand that the daughter and the man had missed.

The giant held out the grains of sand for the man to see and said, "Is this or is this not sand? You lied to me. You sent my daughter to get the water when I told you she was not allowed to do that! Now you die!"

The giant jumped up to kill the man, but the man was too quick for him. He scurried out the door and ran as fast as he could to the giant's neighbor's homestead. This neighbor was also a giant and out plowing his fields.

"Oh, help, help, help!" the man yelled. "Please, please help me! Your neighbor is out to kill me!"

The plowman giant said, "Yes, certainly, stand behind me so I can protect you."

When the cowherd giant arrived, he said, "Where is that little shrimp who made my daughter draw water from the well? Where is he? I promised I would kill him, and I'm here to do it. I know you're hiding him here somewhere!"

The plowman giant replied, "And so what if I am hiding him? He's my friend, and I won't let you hurt him."

At that, the cowherd giant went to a stand of trees growing along the edge of the field. He uprooted one of the trees and came stomping back toward the plowman giant, holding up the uprooted tree like a club.

"Oh, dear," the plowman giant said. "He means to fight. I can't run away because then everyone will think me a coward, and I can't let you loose because he'll surely crush you if he gets the chance."

And so, the plowman giant picked up the man and tucked him into the waistband of his kilt. Then the plowman giant uprooted a tree of his own and went to face the cowherd giant. Such blows were exchanged that day! The sound of the clashing trees was so loud that people miles away wondered whether it was thunder. Not long after the fight had started, the two giants stood panting in the middle of the field, covered with cuts and bruises.

By this time, their giant neighbors had come to see what all the noise was about, and they said, "Now, now, this is no way for neighbors to behave! Make your peace with one another!"

The cowherd giant agreed to go home peacefully and not cause any more trouble, and the plowman giant agreed that he wouldn't restart the fight, either.

Once the cowherd giant had left, the plowman giant sat down to smoke his pipe, for although he had agreed to make peace with the cowherd giant, he was still quite angry and thought that a few puffs on his pipe would help calm his nerves. However, when he reached into his waistband for his pipe and tobacco, he found the broken body of the man, who had been struck and killed by one of the cowherd giant's blows during the battle.

So much for my new friend, the plowman giant thought. It's a pity that he died, but there's nothing I could have done about him being so fragile.

Untombinde and Unthlatu (*Zulu, South Africa*)

This story from the Zulu people of South Africa is set along the mythical river Ilulange, which is home to a monstrous beast capable of swallowing everything in its path. Another not-quite-human character is the prince Unthlatu, who was conceived when a pigeon scratched his mother's side. His mother had to hide him from her jealous neighbors, which she did by wrapping him in a snakeskin. This gives rise to hints later in the text that Unthlatu is himself a snake, or else some kind of creature that is part man and part snake. The story of Untombinde and Unthlatu thus has similarities to the Tutsi story of Gihilihili, retold above.

This story also reflects some important Zulu customs surrounding marriage, which include the bride presenting herself at the groom's family's kraal (family compound) to see whether or not she will be accepted by the groom's family, and the tradition of the bride not eating meat until her wedding feast.

Untombinde and the Monster

King Usikulumi had a beautiful daughter named Untombinde. Untombinde was proud and strong and very tall.

One day, Untombinde went to her father and mother and said, "I would like to go to the river Ilulange. May I have your permission to go?"

"No, certainly not," Untombinde's parents replied. "You know as well as we do that the river is inhabited by a fearsome beast. If you go, you surely will not return, and then what would we do?"

Untombinde obeyed her parents and did not go.

However, the following year, she went to her parents and said, "I would like to go to the river Ilulange. May I have your permission to go?"

Untombinde's parents replied, "You may not go. There is a monster residing there. Surely, if you go, the monster will eat you, and you will be lost to us. You must stay home."

Another year went by, and again Untombinde went to her parents and said, "I would like to go to the river Ilulange. May I have your permission to go?"

Untombinde's parents replied, "We have told you many times of the monster who lives in that river, but if you are still demanding to go there, then go you must."

Untombinde set out on her journey. On the way, she gathered a great following of young maidens who had yet to marry. The maidens and Untombinde traveled along wearing their finest adornments as though they were a wedding party. Along the road, they came across some merchants. The girls parted and lined themselves along the sides of the road to allow the merchants to pass.

As the merchants went by, one of the girls called out, "Merchants! Who among us do you think is the most beautiful?"

The merchants replied, "You are surely beautiful, O maiden, but the most beautiful among you is Untombinde."

At this, the maiden and her friends felt slighted, so they fell upon the merchants and killed them, and when this was done, Untombinde and the maidens resumed their journey.

Soon, the party of young maidens arrived at the river Ilulange. The day was hot, and the sun was bright, so the maidens took off all their finery, leaving it on the banks of the river, and went down to the water to bathe in a place where the river made a little pool. After a time, the girls began to feel that they had had enough of their swim, so the youngest maiden went out of the water to find her clothing and finery. When she arrived at the place where she and her companions had undressed, she found that all their belongings had vanished.

She ran back to the pool, shouting, "Come quickly! Someone has taken away all of our things!"

All the maidens rushed out of the water and went to the place where they had undressed. Just as the youngest maiden had said, everything had disappeared.

"What shall we do?" Untombinde asked. "How shall we find our clothing and our finery?"

One of the girls replied, "This is surely the work of the monster who lives here. We need to go to the monster's place and ask her to give us back our things."

The maidens all agreed that this was the best thing to do, so one by one, they went to the lair of the beast and said, "O great monster who lives in the river Ilulange! Please give me back my clothing and my finery! I came here with the princess Untombinde, and it is she who said we should bathe in this pool. If you do not return our things, surely the princess will call down upon you her father's army!"

Thus, the monster returned the belongings of each maiden until only Untombinde herself was left.

"Untombinde, you must go and ask the monster to give you back your clothing and finery," the maidens said.

"I ask no one. I beg for nothing. I am Untombinde, daughter of the king."

No sooner had Untombinde finished speaking than a hideous monster arose out of the pool. The monster snatched up Untombinde and dragged her down beneath the water. The other girls screamed with fright and called out for their friend, but to no avail. Untombinde did not reappear.

The maidens returned home as quickly as they could and told the king and queen what had happened. "Your daughter bathed in the pool at the river Ilulange, and there she was snatched away by the hideous monster that lives there! Untombinde has been dragged to the bottom of the pool beside the river!"

"I knew this would happen," the king said, and then he called to himself his fiercest and strongest warriors. "Go to the pool at the river Ilulange, where that awful monster lives. Kill the monster and bring back my daughter. Go now!"

The warriors took up their spears and shields and ran to where the monster lived. The monster heard the warriors coming, so it came out of the water to meet them. The monster was as big as a mountain and swallowed up every last warrior. Then the monster went to the king's village and swallowed up all the people there. After it swallowed up the people, it devoured all the animals. When the monster was done devouring, not a single animal was left. Every man, woman, and child had been eaten, except for one man who somehow managed to escape.

Now, this man was the father of twins, and both his children had been eaten by the monster. The man loved his children very much, and he vowed to have his revenge on the foul beast. He took up his weapons and went hunting for the monster. The man walked and walked until he came upon a herd of buffalo.

"Hey, there!" the man called to the buffalo. "Have you seen the monster that ate my village and my children with it?"

"Oh, you are looking for the great monster from the river Ilulange!" the buffalo replied. "Yes, we saw her. She went that way!"

The man thanked the buffalo and continued his hunt.

Soon the man came across a tree in which several leopards were lounging.

"Hey, there!" the man called to the leopards. "Have you seen the monster that ate my village and my children with it?"

"Oh, you are looking for the great monster from the river Ilulange!" the leopards said. "Yes, we saw her. She went that way!"

The man thanked the leopards and continued his hunt.

After journeying on for some miles, the man came across an elephant.

"Hey, there!" the man called to the elephant. "Have you seen the monster that ate my village and my children with it?"

"Oh, you are looking for the great monster from the river Ilulange!" the elephant said. "Yes, we saw her. She went that way!"

The man thanked the elephant and continued his hunt.

It was not long until the man found the monster. She was truly enormous, the size of a mountain, but at that moment, she was crouching on the ground.

The man said, "I am seeking the monster who lives in the pool along the river Ilulange."

The monster replied, "I am that monster. What do you want with me?"

As an answer, the man took his sword and slashed open the monster's side, killing her instantly. Out of the gash in the monster's side came all the people and animals that the monster had devoured. Out of the monster's side came the warriors who had been sent to fight with her. Out of the monster's side came the king and all the maidens who had bathed in the pool. And last of all, out of the monster's side came Untombinde herself, and she was joyfully reunited with her parents.

The Birth of Unthlatu

There was a king named Usibiligwana who had many wives and many sons. One of his wives was the daughter of a very powerful king, but because she had not been able to bear a child, she was thought to be lesser than Usibiligwana's other wives. These other wives mocked her and made her life a misery.

One day, two pigeons came into the kraal. They went to the wife, who had no children, and greeted her.

"What do you want with me, pigeons?" the woman asked.

"Do you have children?" the pigeons replied.

"Alas, I do not."

"Oh, that is sad. What will you give us if we give you a child?"

"I will give you anything I possess. All you need do is ask for it."

The woman showed the pigeons all she possessed, but they refused every last bit of it. "We don't want any of these things. What we want are castor beans. Have you any?"

"Yes, I have a whole pot full," the woman replied.

"Bring it and scatter them so that we may eat."

The woman brought the beans and scattered them for the pigeons.

When the pigeons had eaten all the beans, they said to the woman, "Turn your back to us."

The woman turned, and the pigeons used their sharp claws to scratch deep marks into her loins.

"There," the pigeons said. "Now you will have a son."

The pigeons flew away, and the woman returned to her house, wondering whether the pigeons had spoken truly. Not long afterward, the woman found herself with child and was well content.

Now, several of the other women in the king's kraal were also with child, but when their time came, they gave birth to crows instead of human children. These crows were allowed to stay in the kraal, but they were very unkind to the woman who had spoken with the pigeons. They would go into her house and make all sorts of mischief. If the woman tidied one part of her house, the crows would go and make a mess of it. If she went to fetch water at the river, they would upset the vessels, so she had to go fetch water all over again.

Finally, the day came, and the woman who had spoken with the pigeons felt her pains upon her. She went into her house and delivered a beautiful boy child. She named her child Unthlatu and hid him by swaddling him into the skin of a boa constrictor that had been a gift from her family when she was married.

One day, when Unthlatu was still very young, he came to his mother and said, "Mother, I am in great danger here. I am going away. It is for the best."

Unthlatu left, and although his mother looked high and low for him, she could not find him anywhere. Even though Unthlatu was gone, the mother had a hut built for him in the kraal, and every day she would bring milk, beer, and meat into the hut. Every morning, when the mother went to see whether anyone had eaten the food and drunk the drink, she found that everything had been consumed, but she did not know who was doing it.

Sometimes, maidens would come to the kraal asking to be wed to Unthlatu.

"He is not here," Unthlatu's mother said.

"Where has he gone?" the maidens asked.

"I do not know," the mother replied.

The king invited the young women to stay in his kraal, saying, "After all, I have other sons, even if they are crows."

However, none of the women wished to marry a crow, so they left.

The Wedding of Untombinde and Unthlatu

Now, Untombinde was of an age to be married, so she decided that she would wed Unthlatu, the son of King Usibiligwana. As was customary, Untombinde went to the kraal of Unthlatu's family. She stood there in the kraal, waiting for the bridegroom's family to come and speak to her. She waited for a time, and finally, some members of Unthlatu's family came out to her.

"What are you doing here?" they asked Untombinde.

"I have come to wed Unthlatu," she replied. "He is the son of a king, and I am the daughter of a king, so it is right that we should be wed. Where is Unthlatu?"

At this, the family of Unthlatu cried, "Alas! Unthlatu is not here! He was lost long ago."

When Untombinde heard that Unthlatu was lost, she did not waver. She remained standing in Unthlatu's family's kraal.

Usibiligwana saw Untombinde standing there and said, "Why is that young woman still here? We told her that Unthlatu is gone."

"Yes, we told her," the people replied, "and it would be better if she left."

But still, Untombinde stood in the kraal, waiting.

Again, the king saw Untombinde waiting there, and his heart softened.

"If she wishes to stay, let her stay," he said. "Maybe she will marry one of my other sons instead."

And so, Unthlatu's mother brought Untombinde into the house she had built for Unthlatu. In the house, the mother put milk, beer, and meat, as was her wont.

Untombinde asked, "Why are you putting those things here?"

"This is something I do every evening," Unthlatu's mother replied.

Untombinde watched the mother put the food and drink away. When the mother was gone, Untombinde lay down and went to sleep.

During the night, Unthlatu came to the house. Without waking Untombinde, he ate and drank what his mother had left in the house, and then he left. In the morning, Untombinde woke and saw that the food and the drink had all been consumed.

"Alas! Unthlatu's mother will think I took that food and drink without asking. What will happen now?"

Unthlatu's mother came into the house. She saw that the food and drink had all been consumed.

"Did you eat and drink what I left here last night?" she asked Untombinde.

"No, Mother, I did not touch it," Untombinde replied.

"Did you see who ate it?"

"No, Mother, I saw no one in the night."

The day passed. The people ate and drank. At sunset, Unthlatu's mother again placed sour milk, beer, and meat into the house. Again, Untombinde went to sleep without touching either the food or the drink. In the night, Unthlatu came into the house. He saw Untombinde sleeping there and thought her very beautiful, so he gently caressed her face. Untombinde woke up at his touch.

Unthlatu said, "Why are you here, beautiful one?"

"I am here to be married," Untombinde replied.

"I see. And which young man shall be your bridegroom?"

"I am here for Unthlatu."

"Is he here?"

"No, he is not here. His mother said that he was lost long ago."

"If he is lost, will it not be difficult to marry him?"

"I care not for the difficulty. Unthlatu I will marry, or no one at all."

"Very well. Let us eat meat and drink beer together."

"I may not eat meat or drink beer, for those are wedding foods, and I do not yet have either a bridegroom or a wedding."

Now, all the time that Unthlatu spoke with Untombinde, he was hidden in shadow so that she could not see him. And when day was about to break, Unthlatu left. As soon as it was light, Untombinde went looking for him throughout the house, but she found no one. The food and drink had been consumed as usual—although she had heard no one eat or drink it. Untombinde went to the door and found it fastened tight shut, but she neither heard nor seen anyone come or go, so she began to wonder who or what it was she had been speaking to.

As Untombinde stood there wondering what had happened in the night, Unthlatu's mother came into the house.

"I heard you speaking to someone last night," the mother said. "Who was in here with you?"

"I spoke to no one," Untombinde replied.

"But someone ate and drank the food again. Did you not see who it was?"

"I saw no one."

Again, Unthlatu's mother brought sour milk, meat, and beer and placed them in the house. That night, just as Untombinde was falling asleep, she felt a hand gently caress her face.

"Wake up!" a voice as gentle as the caress said.

It was Unthlatu, returned for the third time.

"Wake up," Unthlatu said, "and touch me. Begin at my feet. Feel me all along the length of my body, from foot to crown, and tell me what my body feels like to you."

Untombinde did as Unthlatu bade her. She touched him at his feet and then felt his legs, torso, and finally his head. His skin was unlike any she had ever touched; it was smoother than human skin and somewhat slippery.

"Would you like to light a fire so you can see me?" Unthlatu asked.

"Yes, I would like that," Untombinde replied.

"Very well, but first, I must take snuff."

Untombinde gave Unthlatu some snuff. He sniffed it in and then spat into a corner of the house. To Untombinde's amazement, the spittle spoke!

It said, "Hail to you, O king! Hail to the great one, the black one, the one as big as a mountain!"

When the spittle had finished speaking, Unthlatu said, "Light a fire, and behold me."

Again, Untombinde did as Unthlatu bade her do. She lit a fire and looked upon her bridegroom. Untombinde saw that Unthlatu's body was both like and unlike a man's. It was a body unlike any she had ever seen, and Untombinde was afraid.

Unthlatu said, "Now you have seen me, but in the morning, you must tell anyone who asks that no one was here with you. I expect that my mother will come to visit you, as I know she has visited in the past. Tell me, what does she say and do when she comes?"

"She weeps because she thinks you are lost forever and wonders who has been eating the food she leaves every day for you," Untombinde replied. Then Untombinde said, "Please tell me where you live and why you left your mother and your people."

"I live beneath the ground. I left because my people wanted to kill me. They knew I was to be made king, and they were jealous. But I think now is the time for me to reveal myself. Go and fetch my mother here so her grief may end."

Untombinde went and fetched Unthlatu's mother. When Unthlatu's mother beheld her son, she wept for joy, but she wept quietly because she did not want the other people to know that Unthlatu had returned.

Unthlatu said to his mother, "What will you now say to my father and the other people?"

"I will tell them I am going to brew beer," Unthlatu's mother replied.

And so Unthlatu's mother went to the king, her child's father, and said, "I am going to brew beer. I am going to brew beer for everyone."

"Why are you going to do that?" the king asked. "What is the occasion?"

"I want everyone, all of our people, to come and see me. I want them to come and see me because I was the queen. I was the queen, and they despised me and threw me away because I had no child. So, I will brew beer, and the people will come to me."

Unthlatu's mother brewed the beer and invited everyone to come and drink it.

The people were very curious as to why Unthlatu's mother would brew beer and invite them, but they also scoffed at her, saying, "Brewing beer won't do anything for her. She's still nothing. She still has no child. What does she think she will gain?"

When the beer was ready, and all the people gathered together, Unthlatu came out of his house. The king and all the people saw his shining, smooth body and were amazed. The people held a great feast to celebrate the shining man. Unthlatu received a leopard's tail, showing that he was now the king. Unthlatu's mother received the tail of a wildcat, showing that she was now dowager queen. Unthlatu was thus restored to his throne, his mother to her dignity, and Untombinde became Unthlatu's wife.

Gihilihili (Tutsi, Rwanda and Burundi)

This story comes from the Central African Tutsi tribe. The tale has all the makings of a good monster story, including a strange and portentous birth, a snake transforming itself into a man, the magical procurement of immense wealth, and a happily-ever-after ending. At the same time, the story is also a fable about the importance of looking beneath the surface and not judging people by their appearance since what initially might look like a monster could turn out to be a kind and handsome prince in disguise.

Once there was a woman who longed for a child. Year after year after year passed, and still, she did not conceive. Finally, when she began to think that she would go to her grave childless, she found herself to be pregnant. She and her husband rejoiced, for they thought their sorrows had finally ended.

The woman went through the normal nine months it takes for a child to grow in the womb, but when the ninth month passed, the woman felt no pains. Then the tenth month passed, and still, the child remained within the mother's womb. More months passed. Then years. Then, one day, the woman found herself stricken with her pains and took to her bed. After a long and difficult labor, she brought the child into the world with the help of her husband. However, when she looked at her husband, joyfully thinking about asking whether the child was a boy or a girl, she saw that the look on his face was one of horror. Then the woman felt a strange sensation move across her thigh, and when she sat up to see what it was, she found that she had given birth to an enormous serpent.

The husband ran out of the house and then ran back in, carrying a shovel.

The husband raised the shovel to strike the snake, but the wife said, "Stop! This creature has done us no harm, and it is still our child. I will not let you hurt him."

The husband put down the shovel and went out of the house again. When he returned, all the village elders were with him. The elders all gathered around the snake and examined it closely. The snake looked at the elders with curiosity, but it did not seem afraid of them.

Finally, the wisest man in the village said, "This creature seems quite harmless. We should treat it well. Take it into the forest. See to it that it has shelter and food. When it comes into its growth, it will shed its skin, and we may learn more about it then."

The husband and wife and the other elders agreed that this was a good plan. The husband built a small but sturdy house in the forest and placed the snake inside it. Every day, the wife cooked good food for the snake, and the husband brought it to the house for the snake to eat.

As the years went by, the snake grew and grew until finally, the time came for it to shed its skin. The snake knew what it had to do. It left the little house where it had thus far spent all its days, and it slithered deep, deep, deep into the forest. There it wriggled and writhed until its skin came clean off, and when it did, there stood a handsome young man, tall and strong and well made in his body. The young man saw his old skin lying there on the forest floor and knew what he must do. He picked up the snakeskin and walked the many miles to his parents' house.

When the parents answered the door, they were surprised to see a strange young man standing there that they did not know.

"Who are you?" the husband asked. "Why have you come here?"

The young man showed the snakeskin to the husband and wife and replied, "I am your child. When I was born, I was in the form of a serpent, but now that I am grown, I am in the form of a man. Look, here is the skin from my previous form. I brought it to prove to you who I am."

The young man's parents were overjoyed that he had returned to them and come back as such a handsome young man. They brought him to meet all the villagers, and soon everyone was gathered around, greeting him and asking him to tell his story, over and over again. The villagers held a great feast to welcome the young man, and everyone was very happy.

One evening, after the day's work was done, the father sat down with his son and said, "My son, you have newly come to us, but you are of an age when you should be wed. Have you given any thought as to which of the young women of the village you would like to be your wife?"

"Yes, father, I have given much thought to that," the young man replied. "When I lived in the forest as a snake, every day I would see the young women come to gather firewood. I would see them go to the river to draw water. And among them was a young woman I knew I would have for my wife, for I loved her from the moment I first saw her."

"Tell me who this woman is."

"It is the daughter of Bwenge, the chief of the village."

The father frowned. "That is impossible. How would we begin to pay the bride price? Bwenge and his family are wealthy. They will expect many riches in exchange for their daughter, but we are poor. We can barely afford to pay even one cow, never mind the many that Bwenge will expect, and we have no gold."

"Never fear, father. I know what must be done. We will be able to pay the bride price. Wait and see."

The young man went outside the house, where he piled up a great deal of wood and lit it on fire. When the fire was roaring, the young man called his mother and father to join him.

"Catch whatever comes out of the fire," he said and threw his old snakeskin onto the flames.

Out of the flames flew bracelets and anklets made of the finest gold, round calabashes, and beautifully woven cloth. Out flew sheep and cattle. Out flew spades and hoes and other useful things. By the time the fire died out, the family was surrounded by a great herd of sheep and cattle and piles and piles of wealth.

In the morning, the father took some of the wealth and went to Bwenge's house to ask for his daughter's hand.

"You may have what I have brought here today," the young man's father said, "and I have more back at my house. My son loves your daughter and would make her a fine husband. If you think him suitable and the bride price sufficient, let them be married as soon as may be."

Bwenge looked at the bride price the young man's family was offering. He looked at the young man.

He thought for a moment and replied, "Yes, the bride price is sufficient, and your son is known to be a good man. He may marry my daughter."

And so it was that Bwenge's daughter and the young man who had been born as a snake were wed. They lived many long and happy years together and had many children. In time, the young man became the chief of that village, and people from near and far would come to seek his wisdom.

No matter what the questioner had asked, the man who had once been a snake would always say, "Do not worry if things do not look right at the beginning. Be patient and kind, and see what will follow from that. And never judge another person by their looks. There may be goodness in them that you cannot see on the surface."

Part III: Damsels in Distress

The Tale of Wanjiru (*Kikuyu, Kenya*)

This Kikuyu tale from central Kenya is one of many world myths that participate in the trope of the young woman going into the land of the dead and being brought back by a young man who loves her. In this case, the young woman is named Wanjiru, and she goes down into a dusty, gray place when she is made a sacrifice to bring rain so that her people may be rescued from a severe drought. One important aspect of Kenyan culture shown in this tale is the way Wanjiru's young man rescues her: He carries her on his back as one would do a child. This is more than just a piggyback ride; it is an intimate way in which the young man shows how he wants to nurture Wanjiru because, in Kenya, mothers usually wear their babies and very young children strapped to their backs in a large, cloth sling.

There came a time when there was no rain. The people all danced and prayed, and prayed and danced, but still, the earth was dry. This happened for one year. Then for a second year. Then for a third year. The crops would not grow, and the cattle became thin and sickly and would give no milk.

"We must have rain!" the people cried. "We must have rain, or we will surely die!"

The people went to the wisest medicine man they could find.

"Tell us what we must do to have rain!" they said. "Tell us what to do, or we will surely die!"

The medicine man agreed to do what he could for the people. He took up his divining tools and cast lots. He cast them well and studied them carefully. For a time, the people thought that maybe he had no answer, and they began to despair.

However, finally, the medicine man said, "Is there among you a maiden named Wanjiru?"

"Yes," the people replied. "We know her well."

"If there is to be rain, you must buy this young woman from her family. Each of you must bring a goat here tomorrow and give it to Wanjiru's family. When everyone has paid their share, the rain will come."

The next day, Wanjiru and her family gathered near the medicine man's house. Wanjiru stood before her father and mother on the dry, flat earth and watched as the villagers approached. Every man and boy in the village was leading or carrying a goat. While Wanjiru stood there silently, the men and boys came up to her family and gave the goats into their keeping. Only a few goats had been given when Wanjiru felt her feet beginning to sink into the ground. She looked down, and indeed her feet had sunk into the parched earth, all the way up to her ankles. As she watched in horror, the earth slowly pulled her down and down. As each goat was given to her mother and father, Wanjiru sank further into the earth.

"Alas!" Wanjiru cried. "Alas, for I am being pulled into the earth!"

Wanjiru's mother and father saw their daughter being pulled into the earth, and they, too, cried out in sorrow, but there was nothing they could do. If they did not accept the goats and let Wanjiru be taken, there would be no rain, and everyone would die.

Just before Wanjiru's upturned face disappeared beneath the ground, she said, "Have no fear. I am going now, but you will have much rain and live long lives."

And with that, she disappeared as though she had never stood on the earth at all.

No sooner had Wanjiru disappeared than dark clouds rolled in, faster than anyone had ever seen them do before. Suddenly, it began to rain. Not the little pitter-pats that start a storm, not the gentle rain that nourishes the crops, but a great deluge. The dry earth drank in the rain, and the people danced all the way to their homes, rejoicing that the rain had come and they would be saved, not caring one bit that they were soaked from head to toe.

Now, although everyone in the village was pleased that Wanjiru had given herself so that they might have rain and live, there was one young warrior who mourned greatly. This fine young man had been in love with Wanjiru and wanted to make her his wife, but he had not yet had the courage to ask her family for her hand. On top of his sorrow, the young man had much anger because Wanjiru's family had given her up without a second thought.

"I will go and find Wanjiru and bring her back from wherever she has been taken," the young man said. "I will find her, and she will be my wife."

The young man took his shield and spear and embarked on his journey. He crossed plains and climbed hills. He walked all the way to the great lake that lay to the west and the great ocean that lay to the east, but still, he could not find Wanjiru. Finally, he returned to the spot where Wanjiru had vanished. He stood on the very place where she had stood, his heart heavy that he could not find her. Suddenly, his feet began to sink into the earth, just as Wanjiru's had done so long ago. The young man was a little frightened but stood firm, knowing that the earth was taking him to find his beloved Wanjiru.

Once the ground had closed over the young man's head, he found himself standing on a dusty road in a dark and barren place. He followed the road, not knowing where it would lead him until he came across a young woman dressed in rags, her body covered in dust. She stood forlornly by the side of the road, her limbs thin, her face full of sorrow. At first, the young man did not recognize her, but when he looked closely, he realized this was his own dear Wanjiru.

"Oh, my dear, dear Wanjiru, how you have suffered to bring us rain!" he said. "Never fear. I will bring you home, and you will be safe and loved again. I will bring you home on my back, like I would a child. Not a step will you have to take. Never fear!"

The young man carried Wanjiru tenderly down the road on his back until he came to the place where he had been pulled into the earth. He felt a tugging at the top of his head, and soon he and Wanjiru were rising back up through the earth. They rose and rose until they found themselves standing in the place where Wanjiru had disappeared so long ago.

"We will wait until it is dark to leave this place," the young man said. "I will take you to my mother's house, where you will be safe. I will keep you from your family because they have behaved very shamefully toward you."

When night fell, the young man carried Wanjiru to his mother's house.

"Who is this that you carry on your back like a child?" the young man's mother asked.

"This is Wanjiru, who sank into the earth to bring us rain," the young man replied. "I have brought her back home, but tell no one that she is here."

Wanjiru lived with the young man and his mother for many months. The young man's mother slaughtered a goat every day and fed the meat to Wanjiru. She made Wanjiru new clothes, and with good food and tender care, Wanjiru soon regained her beauty.

A time came when the village gathered to dance and feast together. The young man brought Wanjiru to the feast, and, at first, no one recognized her.

Then her family saw her and said, "Is this our very own Wanjiru? How did you return to us? What is this miracle?"

However, the young man stepped between Wanjiru and her people, saying, "She should not go with you. You traded her life for goats. You do not deserve her."

Then the young man brought Wanjiru back to his mother's house.

For four days, Wanjiru's parents came to the young man's mother's house, asking to see their daughter. Each time they came, the young man turned them away. But on the fourth day, he relented, and Wanjiru was joyfully reunited with her family. Then the young man and Wanjiru's parents agreed to a proper bride price, and when the young man had paid it, he married lovely Wanjiru, and they lived many happy years together.

The Little Sister with Seven Brothers
(Berber, Morocco)

This Berber tale from Morocco has all the makings of a great fairy tale: Long-lost brothers, a talking cat, a princess restored to her rightful place, and a hideous ghoul that must be defeated. The ghoul is a creature borrowed from Arab folklore and a kind of demon that lives in wastelands, cemeteries, and other uninhabited places. Ghouls are also known for having a taste for human flesh, and the ghoul in this tale is no different.

There once was a woman who had seven children. One after the other, they came into the world, and every single one was male. The woman longed to have a daughter, and the other women in her village taunted her daily because she only ever had boys. The woman loved her sons, but she felt heartbroken that none of her children had been a girl, and she was tired of the abuse she received every time she set foot outside her house.

One day, after her sons were all well grown, the woman found herself again to be with child.

Oh, I hope this will be the daughter I have longed for! she thought and prayed with all her might that God would grant her wish.

When the woman's sons found out their mother was going to have another child, they said to her, "If you wish us to remain with you, you will give birth to a girl. If you have another son, we will leave and seek our fortunes elsewhere. For now, we will go and wait on top of that hill. If the child is a girl, wave a bright piece of cloth. If it is a boy, wave that staff. That way, we will know what we will do."

Now the woman's anxiety was increased twofold, for not only were the women of the village needling her about whether her child would be a boy or girl, but her sons were threatening to leave her if she did not bear a daughter.

Finally, the day came when the woman was to deliver her child. She asked her sister to help with the labor, and the sister gladly did so.

The woman said to her sister, "My sister, when my child is delivered, I need you to stand on the roof of the house and signal my sons. If the child is a girl, wave that bright piece of cloth. If the child is a boy, wave that staff."

The woman's labor was long and painful, but she had great joy in the end, for the baby was a girl. Once the baby was in her mother's arms, the sister went to give the signal. She took the staff, went up on the roof, and waved the staff high in the air so anyone looking toward the house would see her. Whether she took the staff out of spite or because she forgot which item to use to signal the birth of a girl, no one knows, but the effect was the same: The sons saw the staff being waved from the rooftop of their parents' home, and so they left to seek their fortunes in another land.

The mother waited anxiously for her sons to return so that she might introduce their new sister to them, but the afternoon passed, and they did not return. The sun set, and the moon rose, and they still did not return. The night ran its course, and the sun rose, and they still did not return. She waited until the sun was high in the sky, and then she realized that her sister must have waved the staff instead of the cloth and that her sons would not be coming home.

The woman's sorrow at the loss of her sons was tempered by her joy in her new daughter, who grew into a fine, strong girl who was given the name Wudei'a. Whenever Wudei'a went out into the village, people would point at her and laugh, calling her "the little sister with seven brothers." This confused the girl at first since she was the only child in her mother's house, but after enduring many years of this, she began to feel hurt and ashamed.

She went to her mother and said, "Mother, the people in the village keep calling me 'the little sister with seven brothers,' but I am the only child here. Why are the people calling me this? Is it true that I have seven brothers?"

The mother sighed and replied, "Yes, my treasure, it is true. You do have seven brothers. They are grown and left a long time ago to seek their fortunes in other lands."

"I wish to find my brothers. Give me a she-camel and two servants, one male, and one female, so that I may search for them."

The young woman's parents agreed that she should be allowed to go, so they gave her the camel and the servants, along with an enchanted amulet that would let her speak to her parents at a great distance.

The first day of travel went without incident, but on the second day, the manservant said, "Get off the camel and let my wife ride."

Wudei'a called out, "Mother, the manservant wants me to dismount and let his wife ride the camel."

The mother's voice replied through the amulet, "That is not fitting. You stay on the camel, and the servants must walk."

And so, Wudei'a stayed on the camel, for the servants did not know about the amulet, and hearing the mother's voice coming out of nowhere frightened them.

On the third day, the same thing happened: The servants demanded that Wudei'a dismount, but Wudei'a's mother told them that her daughter must ride and the servants must walk.

However, on the fourth day, when Wudei'a called out to her mother, she received no reply, for they had traveled too far, and the amulet's magic was not strong enough to reach back to the young woman's home.

"Right, get off that camel and let my wife ride," the manservant said when Wudei'a's mother did not respond to her calls. "We've had enough of servitude, and your parents can't help you now."

Tearfully, Wudei'a got down from the camel. She walked behind the camel while the manservant's wife rode it. They traveled in this way for many days until finally, they crossed paths with a caravan.

The manservant went to the chief of the caravan and said, "Greetings to you. Can you tell me whether you have seen seven brothers hereabouts? They came from a faraway country and may have settled here."

"Greetings to you as well," the chief replied. "Yes, I know of these brothers. One of them is a sultan, and his brothers govern the provinces. They have a palace in that direction, one day's journey from here."

The manservant thanked the leader of the caravan, and so the three resumed their journey, this time going in the direction the caravan chief had indicated.

When the sultan's palace was just barely visible on the horizon, the manservant called a halt. He forced Wudei'a to strip off her fine clothes and exchange them with the servant's garb his wife was wearing. He also painted Wudei'a's skin with pitch to darken it.

When he was satisfied that Wudei'a had been well disguised, the manservant said, "You have now exchanged places with my wife. You are our servant, and she is your brothers' sister. If you whisper even the tiniest word of this to your brothers, I will surely kill you."

Wudei'a wept at the manservant's words, but she agreed to hold her tongue, for she was afraid and did not want to die.

The trio then resumed their journey, and when they arrived at the palace gate, the manservant told the guard to summon the sultan, for the woman riding the camel was his long-lost sister. Before long, the sultan and his brothers came to the gate and greeted the manservant, who they remembered from the days in their father's house.

The manservant bowed low, and as he helped the false Wudei'a off the camel, he said, "O mighty sultan, I present to you your sister. We have traveled a long way to find you, for you left your parents' home soon after she was born, and she is desirous of meeting you."

"This cannot be true," the sultan said. "We were told that our mother had given birth to another son, and so we left our home."

"Nevertheless, it is true. This woman is your sister, and this girl here is our maidservant."

Now, the brothers knew no reason why the manservant would be dishonest to them, for he had been a member of their parents' household for many years before they left to seek their fortunes. Therefore, they welcomed the false Wudei'a as their long-lost sister and the true Wudei'a as the false one's maidservant. They caused fine quarters to be prepared for their guests, and that evening, there was a great feast to welcome their sister into their palace.

The next day, the brothers decided that instead of going about their business as usual, they would sit with their sister and get to know her. When they heard their supposed sister was still abed, they called the true Wudei'a to them.

"Sit with me and comb my hair," the sultan said, "and tell us tales of our homeland. Tell us of our mother and father and sister."

Wudei'a took the comb and began to comb the sultan's hair and tell tales of her homeland, but this made her so sorrowful that she began to cry quiet tears. One of her tears landed on her arm and washed away the pitch so that there was a white spot amongst the black. When the sultan saw this, he grasped her arm and rubbed at the spot.

When the pitch began to come off, revealing white skin underneath, the sultan said, "Why does the color of your skin change so under your tears?"

Wudei'a replied, "It is because I am your true sister and not the woman who lies abed in the chamber yonder. Our mother never told me about you, but when I learned I had seven brothers, I begged our parents to let me seek you out. They sent me with two servants and a she-camel, but the manservant made me change places with the maidservant and painted my skin with pitch so that you might think I was a servant, too. I am Wudei'a, not that other woman, and you are my true brothers."

The sultan and his brothers became very angry. The sultan took his sword and went to the guest quarters where the servants were and cut off their heads. Then he had his own servants take

Wudei'a to rich quarters of her own, where she was given a hot bath and fine raiment so that she might clean the pitch off her skin and exchange her servant's garb for that of a princess, as was fitting for the sister of a sultan.

The seven brothers spent the next two days in the palace with their sister, but on the third day, they told her they wished to go hunting, which was their favorite pastime.

The sultan said to Wudei'a, "Dearest sister, we are going hunting. Be sure to lock the palace gates behind us, and do not open them for anyone but us. This cat shall keep you company. Make sure that she gets a portion of anything you eat. We will be gone for seven days, and at the end of that time, we will return."

Wudei'a promised to follow her brother's instructions, and when she and her brothers had bidden farewell to one another, the brothers rode out to hunt, and Wudei'a locked the palace gates behind them.

For seven days, Wudei'a followed her brother's instructions. Anytime she took food, she gave a portion to the cat. She did not open the palace gates for anyone. All was peaceful and calm, and on the eighth day, her brothers returned.

"How did you fare, Wudei'a?" the sultan asked.

"Very well, thank you, brother," Wudei'a replied. "I did as you instructed me. I shared all my food with the cat and kept the palace gates locked."

"Were you not frightened?"

"Certainly not. I kept the palace gates locked and the seven doors to my chamber, the last of which is made of iron, all of which were also locked. The cat and I kept good company, and all was well. Is there something I ought to be frightened of?"

"One never knows. The world is a wide place, with many dangers in it. But as long as you follow our instructions by sharing your food with the cat and keeping the gates locked, nothing can harm you. Also, the cat can come and fetch us if you are in danger. She always knows where we are, and so do the pigeons that roost on the kitchen windowsill."

"Oh! You did not tell me about the pigeons. Ought I to feed them as well?"

"Yes, please. If you care well for the cat and the pigeons, they will care well for you."

The sultan and his brothers spent a day and a night in their palace, and in the morning, they took up their weapons and mounted their horses to go hunting.

"We will be gone another seven days," they told their sister. "Mind you follow our instructions. Feed the cat and the pigeons, keep the gates locked, and do not leave the palace."

Wudei'a promised she would do everything exactly as she had been told, and when she had bidden farewell to her brothers, they rode out of the palace gates, which Wudei'a dutifully locked behind them.

Wudei'a then went about the tasks she had to do that day, the cat following her everywhere and watching her every move. While Wudei'a was tidying one particular chamber, she found a bean on the floor. She picked it up and ate it.

"Hang on a minute," the cat said. "Why didn't you share that with me?"

"I'm sorry, I forgot," Wudei'a replied. "Shall I make you some beans? We have plenty in the kitchen."

"No, I don't want those other beans. I wanted half of that bean you just ate, and now I shall show you what happens to people who forget to keep me in mind."

The cat then marched out of the room and into the kitchen, where she urinated on the fire, putting it out entirely. In the evening, when Wudei'a went into the kitchen to cook the evening meal, she found that the hearth had long been cold.

"How did the fire go out?" she asked. "I banked it up well this morning. Mothing should have put out that fire."

"I put it out," the cat replied. "Just goes to show that you should have a care for other people. Good luck making a meal with no fire."

Wudei'a sighed. "You do know that you'll get no food, either, if I cannot cook. But what's done is done. I will have to find a way to rekindle the flame."

Wudei'a looked out the kitchen window, and in the distance, she saw the glow of a fire.

"Maybe that person will be kind and lend me a coal to rekindle the kitchen hearth," she said.

Wudei'a put on her cloak, took up a vessel to carry the coal, and went to the place where the fire was burning. There she saw that it was no person tending the fire but rather a hideous ghoul.

"Greetings, O Ghoul," Wudei'a said. "Would you be so kind as to let me have a coal from your fire? My kitchen hearth is cold, and I have nothing to rekindle it with."

"Would you like a large coal or a small one?" the ghoul asked.

"I'm not sure what difference the size would make, so long as it is alight."

"The difference is this. If you want a large coal, you must give me a strip of your skin from under your ear all the way down to your thumb. If you want a small one, you must give me a strip of your skin from under your ear all the way down to your little finger."

"I may as well have a large coal, then."

The ghoul took a sharp knife and cut away the strip of skin. Then he gave Wudei'a the coal and sent her on her way, her wound dripping blood the whole time.

Now, a raven had seen what happened at the ghoul's fireside, and he thought that the blood trail ought to be covered so that the ghoul could not find Wudei'a again. Thus, the raven hopped behind Wudei'a, who did not know he was there, and wherever the raven found a spot of Wudei'a's blood, he covered it with dirt. When Wudei'a reached the palace gate, the raven flew up behind her and sat on the palace wall, cawing loudly. This gave Wudei'a a start.

She glared at the raven and said, "That was rather rude, you know, frightening me like that. I hope someone does that to you, so you know how it feels!"

The raven cocked its head at Wudei'a and said, "Oh, so this is how you repay my kindness!"

Then it flew off and uncovered the whole trail of blood between the palace and the ghoul's place. Not long afterward, the ghoul decided that he was hungry, and so he set out to find something to eat. He came across the trail of Wudei'a's blood and followed it to the palace gates. He knocked down the gate and searched through the palace until he came to the seven doors that stood between him and Wudei'a's chamber. He stood in front of the doors and called out:

Wudei'a!

Tell me true

what did your grandfather do

the day you left your home?

Wudei'a heard the ghoul's raspy voice and became very frightened. She answered:

He lay abed

Resting his head

Upon a silken pillow.

The ghoul then laughed, broke down the first door, and went away.

The next night, the ghoul came back and asked Wudei'a the same question, and Wudei'a replied with the same answer. Night after night, the ghoul returned, asking the same question, and when Wudei'a answered, he broke down the door until all the wooden doors had been shattered and only the iron door was left standing.

Wudei'a knew that the iron door would not keep the ghoul at bay. She had only one hope: To get her brothers home as soon as possible. Wudei'a took a small scrap of paper and wrote a message to her brothers, begging them to come home as soon as may be, for she was in mortal peril. She tied the scrap of paper to the neck of one of the pigeons.

"Take this to my brothers," she said. "Take it as fast as you can, or I am lost!"

The pigeon flew straight to the brothers' camp, and when they had read their sister's message, they mounted their horses with all haste and rode like the wind back to the palace. There they found the gates broken and hanging open, and the six wooden doors to their sister's chamber in splinters. They had to shout and call to their sister many times before she found the courage to come and open the iron door and let them in. When her brothers entered her chamber, Wudei'a fell into their arms, weeping.

"Oh, dearest sister!" they cried. "What has become of you?"

"I neglected to share one bean that I found with the cat, so the cat put out the kitchen fire, even though I offered to make him a whole bowl of beans for his own. I saw a fire burning in the distance, and so I went to beg for a coal from the person who was keeping the fire, only the person turned out to be a ghoul who demanded a strip of my skin in exchange for the coal. Later that night, the ghoul followed the trail of blood from my wound, and each night since, he has broken down one door and then gone away. I fear that if he breaks down the iron door, he will eat me alive!"

"Never fear, sister," Wudei'a's brothers said. "We will deal with this ghoul, and when we are done, he will no longer be able to hurt you or anyone else."

The brothers then set to work digging a deep pit inside Wudei'a's chamber. At the bottom of the pit, they lit a fire. When that was done, they laid a heavy carpet over the hole. Then they all sat down and waited for the ghoul to come.

That night, the ghoul arrived at the palace at his usual hour. He knocked on the iron door and said:

Wudei'a!
Tell me true
what did your grandfather do
the day you left your home?
Wudei'a replied:
He flayed an ass
Made of it his repast,

Caused fire to burn,

Fell into the flames in turn,

And now he is naught but ash.

When the ghoul heard this, he became very angry and beat down the iron door. In the chamber, he found Wudei'a standing with her seven brothers by her side.

"Welcome," the brothers said to the ghoul. "Won't you sit and have tea with us? Please, sit on that rug there and make yourself comfortable."

Startled to find seven strong young men where he expected to find only one frightened young woman, the ghoul stepped on the rug to take a seat but no sooner had he done so than he fell down into the fire the brothers had prepared earlier. The brothers then heaped more and more wood on the fire until it roared and blazed. When it died down not a trace of the ghoul was left, not even one little hair or scrap of bone, nothing except one paring of a fingernail, which was borne up by the smoke and came to rest on Wudei'a's finger. No sooner had the fingernail touched Wudei'a's skin than it pierced her finger, and she fell to the ground, lifeless.

The brothers cried out in horror and fear. They embraced their sister, calling to her and begging her to wake up, but it was no use. Wudei'a was dead. Weeping, they tied her body to a bier and put it onto the she-camel that had borne her to their palace.

The eldest brother said to the camel, "Camel, take our sister's body to our parents' house. You know the way. Do not stop for anyone or anything unless you hear the word 'shoelace.' Then you should stop and wait to see what happens."

The camel trotted out into the desert, stopping for no one and nothing until she came across three men. Seeing a camel on the loose, carrying a burden, the men decided to give chase, thinking that perhaps there was treasure in the camel's load, but even if not, it was one more camel than they had presently. The men ran after the camel, calling to her and begging her to stop, but still, the camel trotted on, keeping herself just out of reach.

This continued until one of the men said, "Wait a minute, my shoelace has come undone."

No sooner had the man bent to tie his shoelace than the camel came to a halt.

The men took hold of the camel's halter and examined the bier it was carrying. On the bier, they saw the body of a richly dressed young woman with a ring on her finger. One of the men took hold of Wudei'a's hand and pulled off the ring. As he did so, the ghoul's fingernail was dislodged from her finger, and she came back to life.

Wudei'a sat up and said, "May the one who restored me to life have a long life, and may the one who slew me find his own death!"

Hearing this, the camel turned around and trotted back to the palace. For their part, the men were so startled to see a dead woman come back to life that they ran away, thinking themselves lucky to get away with their lives and one very valuable ring. What became of them afterward, no one knows.

The camel bore Wudei'a back to her brothers, who were overjoyed to find that she had come back to life.

"Tell us how this happened!" they said. "We thought you were dead, but here you are, alive again!"

"When we burned the ghoul, one of his fingernails floated up in the smoke and pierced my finger, striking me down. In the desert, some men caught up with the camel and took the ring off my finger. This dislodged the ghoul's fingernail, and once it left my finger, I was alive again."

Wudei'a and her brothers stood together in silence for a moment.

Then the eldest said, "O my sister and O my brothers, I wish to propose a journey to you."

"Speak," the others replied. "Tell us what you wish to do and where you wish to go."

"I think we should go back to our parents' house. They are elderly now, and we should see them again before they die."

Wudei'a and her brothers gladly agreed, and after a journey of five days, they found themselves back in their home village, in the house of their mother and father. It was a joyous reunion, for the mother and father had not thought to see any of their children again, nor did the children think they would ever see their parents. The family spent many happy days together, telling their tales, eating good food, and enjoying being a family once more.

However, not once did the parents ask what led the brothers to leave until, finally, the father said, "Why did you leave? Your mother had a girl child, and you said you would stay if she gave you a sister."

"We left because we were deceived," the eldest brother replied. "Our aunt waved the staff instead of the brightly colored cloth, so we thought the child was another boy. That is why we left. But now all has been put right, and no one will ever deceive us again."

And from that day forward, Wudei'a, her brothers, and her parents lived together with much happiness until the end of their days.

Part IV: Clever Heroes

Ngomba's Magic Basket (Bakongo, Atlantic Coast of Central Africa)

The Bakongo are a Bantu-speaking people who live in what is now Congo, the Democratic Republic of Congo, and Northern Angola. One important feature of this story is the practice of basket weaving, which in Bakongo culture is done with the fibers of the raffia palm. The Bakongo and other related peoples are known for their high-quality baskets and other textiles. However, more important than showing the importance of basket weaving, this tale of a magical young woman who cleverly rescues not only herself but also all the other people who are the victims of a vicious highwayman shows the universal human need to be wanted, loved, and free.

Once there was a young woman named Ngomba. She lived with her mother, father, and three sisters. Ngomba was a sickly girl, whose body was covered with unsightly sores. Everyone made fun of her, and no one wanted her around because the sores made her very ugly.

One day, Ngomba's eldest sister said, "Let's go fishing today."

"Yes, let's," the other two sisters agreed.

Ngomba also replied, "I'm coming, too!"

"No, you are not coming with us," the eldest sister said. "You're sickly and useless. Just stay here where you won't cause anyone any trouble with your unsightly skin."

But Ngomba did not listen. She took up her fishing pole and followed the other three out the door and down the path to the river. When the three elder sisters realized that Ngomba was following them, they turned on her, hit her, and insulted her until she ran away.

Ngomba ran weeping along the river until she could run no more.

Gathering her courage and wiping her tears from her eyes, she said, "I don't need to be with my sisters to catch fish. I can catch them very well all by myself. In fact, I'll catch more than any of them, and then maybe Mother at least will be pleased with me."

Thus, Ngomba cast her line into the water and waited for a fish to bite. As she waited, she sang a song. No sooner had she begun to sing than a fish nibbled on her line. With every line of her song, Ngomba caught a fish and popped it into her creel. This is what she sang:

My name is Ngomba

Nobody wants me

My sisters all hate me

So I have to fish all on my own.

Now, as Ngomba sang her song and caught fish, a highwayman was walking down the road not far from the river. He heard the sound of Ngomba's voice and went to investigate. He watched her sing and fish for a while.

Then he went up to her and said, "Who are you, and what are you doing here?"

Ngomba saw the highwayman and was very frightened.

"Oh, please, please don't kill me!" she cried. "I know I am ugly and covered with sores, but all I want to do is fish and then bring the fish home to my mother. Watch and see how well I can catch fish!"

Ngomba started fishing and singing again, and with every line of her song, she caught a fish and popped it into her creel. This is what Ngomba sang:

Maybe now I will die

And my mother won't even know

But nobody will care

Because I'm all alone

The highwayman watched how quickly Ngomba was able to catch fish and began to think that the young woman could be useful to him.

"Come with me," he said.

"No, I can't do that," Ngomba replied. "I need to bring these fish back to my mother."

"You will come with me, or I will kill you."

Then Ngomba sang,

I guess now I will die

My body laid on a pile of fish

If only Mother had loved me

I wouldn't have come here

And maybe then I could live

And with each line of her song, Ngomba caught another fish and popped it into her creel.

Then she looked at the highwayman and said, "All right, I'll come with you. But only if you can cure whatever is making these sores all over my body."

"Agreed," the highwayman replied, so he took her with him to his home deep in the forest, where she was soon cured of her malady.

It didn't take long before the highwayman fell in love with Ngomba, who was beautiful, clever, and danced very gracefully. The highwayman married her and placed her in charge of all his treasure and the captives he had taken on his raids.

One day, the highwayman came to Ngomba with a long string tied around his waist.

"My wife, take this loose end of the string and hold it tight. The other end is tied to my body. When I am far away, the string will be taut. When I am on my way home, the string will slacken. I wear this so that you will know when I am about to return home so that you won't worry about me."

The next morning, as soon as the highwayman had left for the day, Ngomba gathered all the captives to her and said, "We are going to escape from here and go home to our families. I know how to do this, but I will need your help. First, we need to cut many branches of the palm trees that grow here, and then we need to spread them out to dry. Then we must weave them into a basket large enough to hold all of us."

And so, Ngomba and the other captives went to work cutting the palm branches and laying them out to dry.

They worked until Ngomba felt the string go slack, and when this happened, she said, "Quick! Hide everything. My husband must not know what we are doing. And when he arrives, we must all go to him and greet him with much flattery."

The captives did as Ngomba instructed them. They hid the palm branches, and when the highwayman came home, they all fawned on him, telling him how very glad they were to see him.

The highwayman was very pleased, but he sniffed at the air and said, "Ngomba, my wife, why do you and everyone else smell like palm-tree sap?"

Ngomba began to cry, pretending she was offended. "That's a horrid thing to say to one's wife! I can't bear it. If you say it to me again, I think I shall kill myself!"

"Think nothing of it!" the highwayman said, genuinely alarmed by Ngomba's apparent distress. "Think nothing of it. I'll never say such a thing again. Now, let's eat, and then let's dance together!

Hence, Ngomba, her husband, and the others ate a good meal. When dinner was over, everyone danced, sang, and enjoyed themselves.

In the morning, after the highwayman had left for the day, Ngomba and the others set to work weaving the palm fronds into a huge basket, one that would be big enough to carry everyone.

When the basket was done, Ngomba said, "Now we must see whether it will float. Help me toss it into the air."

Four women helped Ngomba lift the basket. They gave it a gentle push upward. It floated in the air for a time and then came gently back down.

"Good," Ngomba said. "Tomorrow we leave."

Now, the highwayman was not far off, and he was sitting in a tree, waiting to pounce on anyone unlucky enough to be taking the road beneath him. The highwayman saw the basket rise above the treetops and float back down. He thought this a great marvel, but when he went home that evening and smelled palm-tree sap on his wife and the others, he became very angry, for he now knew that Ngomba intended to escape from him and take all the other captives with her.

The highwayman resolved to kill Ngomba that very night as she was sleeping, so he gave her palm wine to drink that had been drugged with a sleeping potion. Once Ngomba was asleep, the highwayman took a slender metal rod and began heating it in the fire, for he had decided to kill Ngomba by sticking the red-hot piece of metal up her nose.

What neither the highwayman nor Ngomba knew was that Ngomba's little sister had felt guilty about the way Ngomba had been treated on the day they went fishing and had followed Ngomba to the highwayman's home in the shape of a cricket. Ngomba's sister now watched the highwayman preparing to kill Ngomba, and she knew that she must do something and do it quickly. So she began to sing a cricket's song. The highwayman was so distracted by the cricket's song that he put down the rod and began to dance, and soon he had forgotten what he had meant to do. However, after a time, the little cricket became tired and stopped singing. The highwayman came to his senses and went back to the fire to heat the rod again and kill Ngomba.

Once the little cricket had caught her breath, she began to sing again, and again the highwayman began to dance, but this time he tried to wake Ngomba to get her to dance with him. Ngomba would not wake; the sleeping potion she had been given was working too well.

"Never mind," the highwayman said. "If you will not dance with me, then I will get everyone else to dance instead."

The highwayman then woke all the captives, forcing them to get dressed and dance until daybreak.

When the rooster crowed, the highwayman went out for the day. Ngomba woke up, the sleeping potion having finally worn off. Ngomba and the others tried to make the basket float again, and when they were satisfied that the magic was working, they collected all the highwayman's loot and put it into the basket. Then they all got into the basket themselves. Ngomba got in last, and once she was inside the basket, it rose into the air and began to float away toward the village where her mother lived.

The highwayman was once more up in a tree waiting to rob whoever passed by, and again he saw the giant floating basket.

"Oh, this is a marvel indeed!" he said and wished he didn't have to sit in the tree waiting for someone to rob because seeing the magical basket made him want to dance so very much.

But then the basket flew closer. And closer. As it passed him overhead, he saw that Ngomba, the captives, and all his wealth were in the basket and floating away from him. The highwayman flew into a rage. Such was his rage that he didn't even climb down from the tree to chase the basket; he simply ran along the treetops until he learned where the basket was going.

The basket floated in the air until it arrived at Ngomba's village. There it landed in front of the house of Ngomba's mother.

Ngomba went running to her mother, crying, "Mother! Mother! I am home safe at last!"

Ngomba's mother came out of the house, wondering what the fuss was about. When she saw Ngomba, she nearly didn't recognize her, for Ngomba had been healed of her malady and now was quite beautiful. But when the mother realized that the young woman who had called out to her was indeed her own dear daughter, she wept with joy and embraced Ngomba tightly. Ngomba told her family everything that had happened and explained who the other people in the basket were.

Just then, the highwayman came into Ngomba's village.

"I'll have you know that this young woman is my wife," he said. "And I'd like her to come back home with me."

"Certainly, certainly!" Ngomba's family replied. "She will go back home with you. But first, we should eat a meal together and dance, for we must thank you for healing her malady and celebrate her visit here today."

Ngomba's mother put a large pot of water over the fire to boil while Ngomba's sisters went and dug a deep pit out of sight of the highwayman. They covered the pit with palm fronds and cloths to make it look like a place for a guest of honor to sit.

When the pit was ready, and the water in the pot was boiling, Ngomba's family said to the highwayman, "Come, sit! We have a place of honor for you!"

However, when the highwayman sat down, the palm fronds gave way, and he fell into the pit. Then Ngomba's family dumped the boiling water on top of the highwayman, so he died.

Ngomba lived happily in her village for the rest of her days, and after dividing up all the highwayman's loot among them, all the other captives were returned to their own families.

Mohammed and the Magic Finger (*Arab, Libya*)

One common fairytale trope is that of the Wonder Child, a child born with special abilities and winds up being the story's hero. In this story, the Wonder Child, whose name is Mohammed, does not have a strange birth—as do many such children in many other tales—but he does have the ability to see things that are very far away and magically know things he should not be able to know. Mohammed is also far cleverer than any of the adults around him and more ruthless than his own ruthless mother.

Once there was a woman who had two children, a son and a daughter. While she was gossiping with the women at the village well, she heard a rumor that there was a town where no one ever died.

What a fantastic story, the woman thought, and for a time, she thought no more of it.

However, over time, the story occupied more and more of her thoughts, so she decided to take her children and look for that place. She searched high and low, and after a long journey, she found a town with no burial ground.

"This surely must be the place!" the woman said, so she and her children settled there.

It was a good place to live, and the woman's children grew up until the son was of an age to marry. He fell in love with one of the town's young women, and so they were wed. Again, the little family lived in peace for some time until one day, the young man felt he would like to make a journey, so he went his way, leaving behind his wife, sister, and mother.

Not much time had passed after the son's departure than the mother said, "I do not feel well. My head hurts terribly. I think I shall go to my bed until I feel better."

The woman's daughter-in-law asked, "Did you say you have a headache?"

"Yes, I said that. Now please excuse me. I must rest."

When the woman had gone to her chamber, the daughter-in-law said that she needed to do some errands in the village, so she left the house. She walked until she came to a butcher shop.

The daughter-in-law said to the butcher, "How much will you give me for my old mother-in-law?"

The butcher replied, "I don't know. I'd have to see her first."

"Come with me." The daughter-in-law led the butcher to her home.

The butchers saw the woman and said, "Yes, we'll buy her."

Then they grabbed her and began dragging her back to their shop.

The woman knew who the men were and was puzzled and afraid. "Why are you laying hold of me this way? What have I done wrong?"

"You have a headache," the butcher replied, "and in our village, we kill people when they fall ill of headache. It is our custom and prevents a lot of suffering."

Seeing that there was no way of either fighting the men or escaping, the woman said, "Very well, but after you kill me, preserve my lungs and liver. These must be given to my son when he returns from his journey."

The butchers and the daughter-in-law agreed, and when the woman had been killed, the butchers gave her lungs and liver to her daughter-in-law, who put them in a safe place until her husband might return.

Now, the woman's daughter had heard all that transpired between her mother and the butchers, and she fled the house, fearing for her life. She ran and ran and ran until she could run no more, and finally, she collapsed onto a large rock beside the road and sat there, weeping. As she sat there weeping bitterly, a man came by.

"What is wrong, young maiden?" the man asked. "How may I be of help?"

"Oh, sir, my mother has been killed, and my brother is far away on a journey. I am afraid I will be killed, too, and I have no one to protect me."

"If you come with me, I will see to it that you are safe. Will you come?"

"Gladly," the young woman said.

Thus, they journeyed on to the man's home, which was reached by a long tunnel that went deep into the earth. At the end of the tunnel, a great city had been dug out of the rock. The man brought the young woman into his home and treated her well, and in time, they decided to be wed. They lived together happily and had a son, who they named Mohammed.

Now, this Mohammed was an unusual child. He had a magic finger. If he held his little finger in front of him, he could see as far away as a man could travel in two days. The people of the village often asked him to look for relatives and friends who were on journeys so that he might tell them how they fared.

Meanwhile, as little Mohammed grew into a fine boy, his uncle returned from his journey.

He went to his wife and said, "My mother and sister are not here. What has become of them?"

His wife replied, "Come and sit and refresh yourself. Then I will tell you what became of them."

The man immediately became suspicious. "I will not refresh myself until I know what happened to my mother and sister. Tell me at once."

"Well, your mother had a headache, so I sold her to the butcher for this box of money." She showed her husband a small chest full of gold coins. "She asked that her liver and lungs be saved for you, and I have them here. As for your sister, she ran away while the butchers were here, and I don't know where she went. I haven't heard anything of her since."

"Give me my mother's liver and lungs at once."

The wife gave the liver and lungs to him.

He wrapped them in a cloth and said, "I bid you goodbye forever. This is a horrible place, and you are all horrible people. I am leaving and will never return."

Now, back in the city under the earth, little Mohammed was holding up his finger to see what might be seen, as was his wont.

He spied his uncle in the far distance, so he ran to his mother and said, "Mother! Mother! My uncle is on his way here! I just saw him!"

"How far away is he?" Mohammed's mother asked.

"Oh, he is quite far, two days' journey at least. But he is coming to us, that is certain."

And so it happened that two days later, the young man found the hole that led to the city under the earth. He went down the path to the city, his clothes in rags, his shoes nearly worn through, and not a penny in his pocket, for he had spent everything he had searching for his sister. He sat in front of the city gates, thinking that he would beg a crust or coin from whoever happened to pass by, when suddenly, a young boy came running up to him, leading a woman by the hand. The young man's heart swelled in his breast, for he recognized his sister and stood to greet her and her son.

"Here he is! Here he is!" the child cried. "Here is my uncle. See? I told you he would come!"

Brother and sister threw their arms around one another and wept while the child jumped up and down with joy.

"Brother, please come home with us," the young woman said. "You look weary and hungry, and we have much to tell each other."

The three went back to the young woman's home, and when her brother had eaten and refreshed himself, she told him her tale, of how the butchers had come for their mother and how she had run away since there was nothing she could do to save their mother and she was afraid for her own life.

"Now tell me your tale, brother," the young woman said. "How did you find us?"

"Entirely by chance," the brother replied. "After I learned of our mother's death, I left that horrible village behind and wandered the world looking for you. Your son apparently saw me and knew me for your brother—although how he managed that, I do not know."

"Oh, my little Mohammed has a great gift. If he holds his finger out in front of his face, he can see things up to two days' journey away. He was looking about him with his magic finger one day and saw that you were coming, so he kept watching and let me know you had arrived."

The sister invited her brother to stay with them, and he did, having nowhere else to go. Now, the sister had not told her brother the whole truth about her family. She had not told him that her husband was both very wealthy and also a shape-shifter. Her husband could turn himself into all manner of monsters and foul beasts whenever he wished, and the sister hatched a villainous plot against her brother.

The sister did not put her plan into motion immediately. Instead, she first asked her brother whether he might take their sheep out to pasture.

"Certainly," the brother said, who wished to repay his sister and brother-in-law for their kindness toward him.

The brother took the sheep out that morning and returned them dutifully in the evening. The next day, the sister asked her brother to take the goats out.

"I'd much rather take the sheep," he said.

However, his sister told him that the goats needed to go to pasture that day, not the sheep, so the brother took the goats out.

While the brother was out in the pasture with the goats, the sister went to her husband and said, "Husband, I want you to kill my brother. I don't want him living here with us."

"That is a strange thing to ask," the husband replied. "Your brother seems to be a good man. I don't know why I should harm him."

"You will do as I say, or I will leave you."

"Very well. What must I do?"

"Tomorrow, after my brother has left for the day, transform yourself into a serpent. Put yourself into the date barrel. I will tell him to get himself some dates, and when he puts his hand in the barrel, you must bite him, and then he will die from your venom."

In the morning, the brother bade farewell to his sister, saying that he would take the goats out to pasture.

"Uncle, take me with you, please," little Mohammed said.

"If your mother agrees, certainly," the young man replied.

"Yes, you may go," said the sister. "But mind your uncle!"

Hence, it was that Mohammed and his uncle went out together with the goats, and once the goats were busily grazing, Mohammed said, "Uncle, you are in great danger. I heard my mother and father talking, and my mother told my father to transform himself into a serpent and hide in the date barrel. She intends to tell you to get some dates to refresh yourself, and my father is to bite you when you reach into the barrel."

"Oh, how terrible!" the young man cried. "What am I to do?"

"Never fear, uncle. I will help you. When my mother tells you to get some dates, tell her that you're not feeling well, and ask me to get the dates for you. My father won't bite me, and you will be safe."

That evening, when the young man and Mohammed returned to the house, the sister said, "You look tired and hungry, brother. Please help yourself to some dates from that barrel over there."

Remembering what Mohammed had told him, the young man said, "Thank you, Sister, but I am too tired to fetch them for myself. Perhaps Mohammed here can get them for me."

"Yes, uncle!" the boy said, who ran over to the barrel and opened the lid.

"No, Mohammed, let your uncle get his own dates!" his mother said.

"It is no trouble, mother." Mohammed put his hand into the barrel and whispered, "Do not bite me, Father. It is I, Mohammed, your son."

Mohammed pushed his hand past the cool, soft skin of the snake and grabbed a handful of dates, which he brought to his uncle. The young man ate the dates gratefully, for he actually was quite hungry, but he also was glad that little Mohammed had kept him out of danger.

When the brother retired to his chamber, the husband slithered out of the barrel and turned back into a man.

"It is good that I did not kill him," the husband said. "He really has done us no harm at all."

"I don't care about that," the young man's sister replied. "I want him dead, and you will kill him, or I will leave you."

"Very well." The husband sighed. "I will try again tomorrow. This time I'll hide in the straw of his bed."

In the morning, the sister told her brother, "Brother, it is time to take the goats out to pasture."

"I'm going, too!" little Mohammed said.

"No, you are not. You will stay right here with me."

But Mohammed began to cry and stamp his feet and make such a scene that his mother relented, so the young man and his nephew took the goats out to the pasture together.

When they arrived at the pasture, Mohammed said, "My parents will try to kill you again when we get home. This time, my father will hide in the straw of your bed. I will help you, but you must trust me. This time I will kill my father myself."

The young man agreed to follow his nephew's lead.

When they got home that evening, the sister said, "Brother, the straw of your bed is old and should be refreshed. Why don't you feed it to the sheep and replace it with fresh straw?"

"Let me! Let me!" Mohammed said.

"No, you are not big enough for this task," his mother replied. "Your uncle must do it."

"We can do it together. Come, uncle. Let us refresh the straw of your bed."

Together, the boy and his uncle went to the uncle's chamber.

They stopped in the doorway, and the boy said, "It is terribly dark in here. We won't be able to see a thing. Let me go and get a light."

The boy fetched a taper from the kitchen, and with it, he set the straw alight, burning his serpent father to a crisp. The mother heard the sound of the flames and smelled the smoke, and came running.

"Oh, what have you done?" she cried. "What have you done? Your father was in that straw, and now he is dead!"

"How was I supposed to know he was in there?" the boy asked. "I did not mean to harm him. I tripped and fell when I went into the room and dropped the taper. It set the straw alight. It's his own fault, anyway, since he had no place being there."

"Oh, you wretched, wretched boy! Now you have no father. What are you going to do about that?"

"I don't see that I can do anything at all, but I find it strange that you married a serpent. And all this time, I thought my father was a man!"

In the morning, the sister once again asked her brother to take the goats to pasture, and once again, Mohammed went along with his uncle.

When they arrived at the pasture, Mohammed said, "Uncle, tonight my mother plans to poison the both of us. She will take the serpent-bones of my father, grind them to a powder, and put them in our food."

The uncle sighed. "I seem always to be in danger, and I have no idea how to get out of it."

"Never fear, Uncle. I will take care of everything."

Uncle and nephew drove the goats back home that evening, and when they went into the house, they found that the sister was preparing food for the evening meal.

"Go and wash your hands," she said, "and when you return, dinner will be on the table."

The uncle and nephew went to wash their hands, and while they were about that business, the boy said, "Uncle, pay close attention to what side of the dish I take my food from. Be sure to take yours from the same side, for my mother only put the poisoned powder on one side so that she can eat the same dish and not be harmed."

The three sat down at the table.

The sister said, "Please, help yourselves."

The boy replied, "Wait, Mother, may I first have a cup of milk to go with my dinner?"

"Certainly," the mother replied.

When she left to get the milk for her son, Mohammed served himself and his uncle from the side of the dish that had not been poisoned and then positioned the dish to make it look like they had taken from the poisoned side. Accordingly, when the sister came back with the milk and served herself and began to eat, she dropped down dead instantly, for she had taken the poison she meant for her brother and son.

"There, that's done," the boy said. "I'm glad she and my father are dead. They were both horrible people, and they deserved what they got. Now, let's sell all the herd animals, and when that is done, we can go and travel the whole world."

Uncle and nephew traveled all about, seeing many wondrous places until, one day, they came to a fork in the road.

Mohammed said, "Uncle, we must now go our separate ways. Tell me what way you would prefer to go?"

"No, we must not part!" the uncle replied. "I owe my life to you and would not be parted from you for anything!"

"I would stay with you if I could, but this is how it must be. So, tell me, what way will you go?"

"I will go west."

"Very well. However, before we part, I have one more important thing to tell you, and you know my advice is very good. If you choose to go into anyone's service, that is well—unless it is for a man with blue eyes and red hair. Him you must avoid at all costs, but for anyone else, you may work without trouble."

Then uncle and nephew embraced one another and said their tearful farewells before each went his own way.

Now, the money that Mohammed and his uncle had made from the sale of the herd animals was already running low when the two of them reached the crossroads. It did not take long before the young man found himself penniless and very hungry indeed. He lay down at the edge of the road, unable to go any farther and lamenting his fate when a red-haired, blue-eyed man came and stood over him.

"You seem to be in a bad way," the red-haired man said. "Are you in need of work?"

"I am indeed," the young man replied. "What are your terms, and will we have a written contract?"

"In exchange for food and shelter and two coppers a day, you must do three things every day. You must herd my sheep and take them out to pasture. You must carry my aged mother about on your back, never letting her feet touch the ground. And you must capture seven songbirds to bring home as gifts for my seven sons. And yes, we can put the contract in writing, if you like."

"Very well. And if either of us breaks this contract, what is to happen?"

"The one who breaks our agreement will have a strip of skin flayed from his body."

Seeing that his choice was either to accept the man's terms or starve, the young man signed the contract and went home with his new employer, who introduced him to his mother and sons and showed him where the sheep pen was.

"Tend to your duties," the red-haired man said, and so the young man took the old woman upon his back and herded the sheep out to the pasture.

While the sheep were grazing, the young man caught seven songbirds and put them into his pockets. In the evening, the young man drove the sheep back to their pen, carrying the old woman on his back the entire time. Then he gave the songbirds to the children and retired to his chamber, where he ate the meager food the red-haired man gave him.

And so the young man's days went by, one after the other, doing the same arduous tasks for the same terrible food and terrible pay until, one night, he could stand it no longer and began to weep and lament his fate.

From afar, Mohammed saw his uncle's sorrow and resolved to do something to help him.

Mohammed had also accepted employment as a servant, so first, he went to his employer and said, "Sir, I have had word that my uncle is in a very bad way, and I must help him. I would like to send him here to work for you, and I will work for his employer for a time. When my uncle arrives, you will know I have sent him because he will carry my staff and wear my cloak."

Mohammed's employer gave his permission and promised to watch for the uncle and take him into his service when he arrived. Then Mohammed went to the village where his uncle was living. He saw his uncle out in the pasture, running about trying to catch songbirds with the old woman on his back.

Mohammed went up to his uncle and said, "Uncle! Whatever are you doing?"

"I am doing the tasks my employer has set me," the young man replied.

"And does this employer have red hair and blue eyes?"

"Yes, he does."

"Uncle, did I not tell you to avoid that man at all costs?"

"You did, but I was desperate and about to die. I had no other choice, and now we have a written contract between us that both of us have signed."

"Give the contract to me. We will exchange places. I will work for your employer, and you will work for mine. Take my staff and my cloak. I told him to watch for you, and he has agreed to take you into his service. You will find him two days' journey from here, along that road. Now, put that old woman down, and be on your way."

"I cannot do that, for the contract says that if I do not perform my duties, the red-haired man can flay a strip of skin off my body!"

"Never mind that," said Mohammed. "Haven't I gotten you out of trouble every time before this? So, put the woman down and go to my employer. I will set all to rights here."

"Very well." The uncle put down the old woman and walked away down the road his nephew told him to take.

Once the uncle was on his way, Mohammed picked up a switch and swatted the old woman with it.

"Now you work for me, you old hag," he said. "Look after the sheep. I'm going to take a nap."

"Very well," the old woman replied.

Thus, the day passed with the old woman looking after the sheep and Mohammed snoozing away in the shade of a large tree.

When the sun began to set, Mohammed woke and said, "Hey, old woman! Did you catch the birds yet?"

"You only told me to watch the sheep," she replied. "You said nothing at all about birds."

"Oh, dear. We can't go back without the birds. You'll just have to catch them now, and if you don't, I will kill you."

The old woman rushed to catch the birds, but she was wearing no shoes, and so her feet were pierced by many thorns when she went into the bushes to catch the birds. When all the birds had been caught, Mohammed and the old woman headed back to the house with the sheep.

"You will have to drive them," Mohammed said. "I do not know where they are supposed to go. And be warned: If you say anything about my making you herd the sheep or catch the birds, or if you say anything about my having traded places with my uncle, I will surely kill you!"

The old woman was terrified and so readily agreed not to say anything. When the pair got home and had put the sheep into the fold, they went into the house.

The red-haired man said to the old woman, "We have a fine shepherd, do we not?"

The old woman replied, "Oh, yes, he is a very fine shepherd indeed!"

When the evening meal had been prepared, Mohammed told the old woman, "You are not to eat until I have had my fill. You can have whatever is left over after I eat, and if you say anything to your son, I will kill you."

The old woman wept at this, but she was frightened and so did as Mohammed told her.

In the morning, Mohammed took the old woman on his back and drove the sheep out to pasture. When they arrived at the pasture, he put the old woman down, took a ram, and slaughtered it. Then, he made a fire and began to cook some of the meat. When the meat was done, he called the old woman over to share the food. The woman came over to the fire, but instead of handing her a portion of the meat, Mohammed took a great chunk of it and forced it down her throat so that she choked and died.

"That is your reward for treating my uncle so shamefully," Mohammed said.

Mohammed then went into the bushes to catch the seven songbirds. When he had all seven sewn up in his clothing, he herded the sheep back to their fold. Just before he came into sight of the house, he began to weep. The seven children came running out to greet him and receive their gift of the songbirds.

They saw that Mohammed was weeping and said, "What is the matter? Why are you crying?"

"Oh, it is the most terrible thing!" Mohammed replied. "Your grandmother is dead. She told me to kill a ram so she might cook us a meal, but when she took some of the meat, she choked on it!"

The children ran and got their father, who made Mohammed tell his whole story over again.

"Why did you kill the ram?" the red-haired man asked when Mohammed had finished his tale.

"I had to follow the old woman's orders," Mohammed replied. "I had no choice."

Then Mohammed told the red-haired man where he had left the old woman's body since the man wished to see his mother's proper burial.

In the morning, Mohammed went out with the sheep as usual. On the way, he thought about how he was to deal with the seven children. When he arrived at the pasture, he looked for songbirds as usual, but instead of catching seven, he only caught one. At the end of the day, he began digging small holes in the ground, and in the holes, he found six scorpions. He carefully put the scorpions into his pocket and drove the sheep home. When the children came out to receive their birds, he gave scorpions to all but the youngest, and the youngest received a bird. All six elder children were stung by the scorpions and died.

When the red-haired man came out to see what was wrong with his children, Mohammed said, "It couldn't be helped! This time of year is so cold, and the children's fingers were stiff and unable to hang onto the birds I gave them, and their spirits went into the birds and flew away. That is why they are dead. Only the youngest managed to hold onto his bird. That is why he is still alive."

The red-haired man wept over his dead children and said, "Enough. Bring no more birds. I do not want to lose my last child."

In the morning, Mohammed said, "I have discovered a pasture with even better grass than the one you told me to use, but it is several days' journey from here. May I have leave to go there? I will bring the sheep back much fatter than they are now, you will see!"

The red-haired man agreed, but, of course, Mohammed had no intention of going to a different pasture. Instead, he drove the flock to where he had left his uncle.

"Uncle, here is the flock of the red-haired man. Take it for your own in payment for what he did to you. Wait for me here a while longer, for I have other things yet to do."

Mohammed set out for the red-haired man's house, and when the house was not far, Mohammad took a sharp rock and hit himself in the face with it.

Then he bound his hands tightly with a bit of cord and ran the rest of the way to the red-haired man's house, crying, "Master! Master! Oh, help me! Brigands set upon me and took the sheep. I managed to escape, but not before they had beaten me."

"Which way did they go?" the red-haired man asked.

"It's no use trying to follow them. This happened several days ago. They'll be long gone. I came home as fast as I could."

"Very well. From now on, you will herd the cows instead."

In the morning, Mohammed took the cows out to pasture. There he cut off the tails of all but one cow and drove all but that one cow to where his uncle was staying.

"Dear uncle, please take these cows in recompense for what the red-haired man did to you. I pray you continue to wait for me here. I will return as soon as I can."

Mohammed then went down to the seashore, where he buried the tails in the sand with the tufts sticking out. Then he fetched the one cow he had left in the pasture and buried her in the sand, too, with only her head and the tuft of her tail sticking out. Screaming and crying, Mohammed ran back to the red-haired man's house.

"Master! Master!" he cried. "Come quickly! The sea has swallowed up all your cows! Please come and help me get them back!"

The red-haired man shouted for some other farmhands to come along, and soon, he and his servants arrived at the seashore, where they started pulling on the cut-off tails that Mohammed had buried.

"Oh, dear!" Mohammed said. "That's not the way to go about that. All you've done is pull off their tails, and the rest of the cow is now down at the bottom of the sea."

"How would you do it?" the red-haired man asked.

"Like this." Mohammed went and pulled out the one whole cow he had buried.

The red-haired man glowered at Mohammed and said, "Go away from me. You have been nothing but trouble since you left. Now that my children and mother are dead and my herds are all gone, there is no reason for you to continue working for me. Begone!"

"I will go, but first, you must give me a strip of your skin. That was part of the contract."

"After all you have taken, you still want that, too?"

"Yes, and if you do not give it to me here, then let us go before a judge and have him decide the matter."

And so, Mohammed and the red-haired man went before a judge, and each pleaded their case. In the end, the judge decided that the red-haired man owed Mohammed a strip of his skin, so the red-haired man took a knife, carved a strip out of his arm, and gave it to Mohammed.

Mohammed then returned to where his uncle was and showed him the bit of the red-haired man's skin. Then the pair sold off all the sheep and cattle, so they had a great deal of money.

"Now we can resume our travels," Mohammed said.

In the morning, the pair set off down the road together.

One evening, they stopped for the night at a Bedouin encampment. The leader of the group of Bedouins invited Mohammed and his uncle to dine with them.

Mohammed said to the leader, "Thank you for your hospitality, but I have a strip of skin here that is very precious to me. Are you sure your hound is well trained and that he will not eat it?"

"My hound indeed is well trained," the leader replied. "Never fear."

"But what if your hound eats it anyway?"

"Then I will give him to you in recompense."

That night, Mohammed took the piece of skin and fed it to the hound.

"Alas! Alas!" he cried. "The hound has eaten my precious strip of skin! I knew this would happen! Alas!"

The leader of the encampment came running, and Mohammed told him about the hound eating the piece of skin.

"You must now give me your hound," Mohammed said. "You promised."

The Bedouin chief put a leather cord around the dog's neck and handed the long end to Mohammed. "There, he is yours. Now get out of my camp before any other misfortune befalls."

Mohammed and his uncle journeyed on until they came to another Bedouin encampment.

The leader invited them to spend the night there, and Mohammed said, "Thank you for your hospitality, but I am concerned that your ram will kill my hound."

"Oh, I doubt that will happen," the leader replied. "But if it does, you may have my ram in exchange."

That night, Mohammed killed the dog and put it in the pen with the ram, smearing some of the dog's blood on the ram's horns.

Then Mohammed began to cry out, "Alas! Alas! The ram has slain my hound! Alas!"

Hence, the leader gave Mohammed the ram and told them to leave the encampment before more misfortune befell.

On and on, Mohammed and his uncle journeyed until they came to a third Bedouin encampment, where they were again invited to pass the night.

"Thank you for your hospitality," Mohammed said. "But I am worried that your daughter might kill my ram."

"That is preposterous," the leader replied. "Why would she do such a thing?"

"I am sure I do not know, but what will you give me if it happens?"

"I will give you my daughter in exchange for your ram," the leader replied, and Mohammed agreed.

That night, when all were asleep, Mohammed killed the ram. He took its liver and put it in the hand of the leader's sleeping daughter and then sprinkled some of the ram's blood over her.

Then he began to wail and cry out, "Alas! Alas! This maiden has slain my ram! What is to be done!"

The leader came to his daughter's tent and saw the bit of liver and the blood. He became very angry.

"Get out of my camp," he said to her. "You are a disgrace to me. You belong to this man now. Get out!"

Mohammed and his uncle resumed their journey, the young woman traveling with them. At nightfall, they came across another Bedouin encampment, where they were invited to pass the night.

Mohammed said to the camp's leader, "Thank you for your hospitality, but I am afraid that your mare will kill my wife."

"That seems most unlikely," the camp leader replied. "But if it happens, you may have the mare in exchange."

That night, Mohammed woke the young woman and said, "Do not be afraid. I have a plan that will be of benefit to us all. I must make a few cuts in your skin and smear the blood all over you. You must lie very still, as though you are dead. Do not move or make a sound, or it will go the worse for all of us."

The young woman agreed, and when all was ready, Mohammed began to wail and cry out.

"Alas! Alas! The mare has killed my wife, my darling wife! Oh, how will I ever live without her?"

The Bedouin leader came running and said, "Fine, take the mare and go. Bring the woman's body with you. Now get out!"

Mohammed and his uncle draped the young woman over the mare's back, and the young woman pretended to be dead the entire time. They walked down the road until the Bedouin encampment was well behind them, and then the young woman sat up.

"I am hungry," Mohammed said, "and I am sure the both of you are as well. Let us rest here."

The three took shelter in the shade of a tree and refreshed themselves with dates and a little water.

Then Mohammed said, "Uncle, I give this young woman to be your wife. I myself will never marry. Let us also take the money we got from selling the cows and sheep. You take two-thirds for your own and give me one-third. Then I must leave you, for I have my own journeys to make, and you will never see me again."

Uncle and nephew embraced and bade one another a tearful farewell. Then they parted, each going his own way.

Walukaga and the King's Request
(*Baganda, Uganda*)

Many African cultures have long traditions of metalworking. Evidence shows that the smelting and working of iron in Central Africa may have begun as long ago as 2000 BCE. This Baganda story about a blacksmith named Walukaga gives some evidence of the high regard in which workers with iron could be held, but it is also a parable about the importance of not asking for impossible things.

Once there was a master blacksmith named Walukaga. Such was Walukaga's skill and reputation that one day the king sent a messenger to Walukaga's forge.

The messenger said, "The king summons you. He has a task to give you. You must come right away."

Walukaga was honored that the king wanted his services, but he was also a bit anxious. What if the king asked him to make something that Walukaga did not know how to do? However, Walukaga put those thoughts aside and went straight to the king's home, wearing his very best clothing.

When Walukaga arrived, the king said, "Welcome. I have heard that you are the best blacksmith in the world and can make things that other people cannot. I wish you to make something for me that everyone will know to be the most marvelous thing in the world."

"Tell me what you desire, Your Majesty," Walukaga replied, "and I will do my very best for you."

"I want you to make a man out of iron."

"That is easily done. I have made many such statues."

"Oh, but this one will be different. I want it to be the same height as a man. I want it to walk and talk. I want it to have much wisdom so that it can advise me and help me to rule my kingdom."

Walukaga blinked and stood mute. He knew that what the king asked was impossible, but it was also impossible to say that to the king.

So, instead, Walukaga said, "I will do my best, Your Majesty. Have you a quantity of iron for me to work?"

The king gave Walukaga a great quantity of iron, and back at his forge, Walukaga racked his brains trying to find a way to make the iron man the king had asked for. Walukaga asked all his friends and neighbors for advice, but no one could tell him what to do. They all agreed on one thing, though: Walukaga would likely be punished if he didn't give the king what he wanted.

One day, Walukaga had occasion to make a journey through some wasteland inhabited by a madman. Walukaga had known the man before he went mad and did not know that the man was now living in this wasteland. The man saw Walukaga walking down the road and went to greet him.

"Welcome, Walukaga, old friend!" the madman said. "How are things with you?"

Walukaga recognized the man and greeted him in return.

Then Walukaga said, "Things aren't very well with me, I'm afraid."

"Tell me your troubles. Maybe I can help."

"The king commissioned me to make a man out of iron. He wants it to be life-size. But that's not the problem. The problem is that he wants the iron man to walk and talk and be wise so it can advise the king. It will not be possible to make such a thing, but if I don't make it, the king will punish me, and I am afraid."

"Yes, that is a difficult problem. However, I think I know what you should do. Tell the king that to make the iron man, he will first need to ask all his subjects to shave off their hair. Then the hair needs to be burnt to make charcoal. When enough hair has been collected and burnt to make a thousand loads of charcoal, you will have enough. Then tell the king that for the hair not to burn too long and spoil the charcoal, you will need a hundred pots of tears collected from all the kingdom's subjects. Tell the king that if he wants a special iron man, then nothing less than special ingredients need to be used."

Walukaga thanked his friend for his good advice, went to the king, and told him that he needed the charcoal made out of hair and the pots of tears to make the iron man. The king ordered all his subjects to shave their heads, but when the hair was burnt, there was not even one whole load of charcoal made, and no matter how hard the king's subjects wept, he could not collect more than two pots of tears.

The king sent for Walukaga and said, "I did what you told me to do, but as you see here, there is only part of one load of charcoal and two pots of tears. I suppose you won't be able to make me the iron man after all."

"No, Your Majesty, I won't be able to make the iron man you wanted," Walukaga replied. "It was an impossible task from the beginning, which is why I asked for the charcoal made of hair and the pots full of tears, so you would understand that it could not be done."

And so, such a tale teaches us the life lesson of not asking for or expecting something that is, in truth, impossible to achieve.

Free Bonus from Captivating History (Available for a Limited time)

Hi History Lovers!

Now you have a chance to join our exclusive history list so you can get your first history ebook for free as well as discounts and a potential to get more history books for free! Simply visit the link below to join.

Captivatinghistory.com/ebook

Also, make sure to follow us on Facebook, Twitter and Youtube by searching for Captivating History.